THINGS MY MOTHER DIDN'T TEACH ME

Raising a child with equal amount of care and nurture

LINNET DAVE

Made with ♥ on the Notion Press Platform
www.notionpress.com

Contents

Preface

In her essay "The Role of Women in Society",
Amrita Pritam writes:

"Women are the backbone of society.
They are the ones who raise our children,
care for our elderly,

And keep our homes running.
We must give women their due respect,
and ensure that they have equal rights."

(Source: Sikkim Express)

Coexistence is the key to growth and harmony in every society. While women are an embodiment of power, it manifests in the form of sacrifice, submission, and subdued emotions. This manifestation is interpreted as heroism. But a society where women thrive, not because they sacrifice or choose to be submissive, but rather endeavour to speak for themselves and live the life they choose, can be called progressive.

Women creating success stories amidst resistance and lack of support need not be an axiom. When women speak for themselves, they should get support from other women.

A comradeship among women is so necessary, which is possible by instilling self-belief. Let's act as catalysts in the success stories of other women, supporting, acknowledging, and thriving, based on collective power.

As I have kept pondering upon this thought for a long time, during COVID-19 pandemic, I read about the significant impact of the pandemic on women.

COVID-19 didn't favour women as they were at home, juggling housework and professional commitments. They were clearly overburdened.

During the pandemic, Auxano Consulting studied 'Gender-Biased Workforce and its Impact on the Industry.' The revelations on labour force participation were alarming.

Women spent more time performing unpaid work, such as childcare and housework, than men.

Globally, only 41 million (1.5%) men provide unpaid care on a full-time basis compared to 606 million (21.7%) women.

On average, across the globe, women spend 4 hours and 22 minutes per day in unpaid labour, compared to only 2 hours and 15 minutes for men.

COVID-19 worsened the situation for women and widened this gap even further. Women were spending 15 hours more in unpaid labour each week than men.

Women were exhausted during the pandemic. They took care of their homes, children, and families. One in three women across the world face physical and sexual violence, mostly from an intimate partner, as mentioned by UN Women and considered a human rights violation.

During the pandemic, reports reflect an alarming increase in different types of violence against women and girls, particularly domestic violence, have risen.

The National Commission for Women (NCW) India released a study in early April 2020, that mentioned a 100% increase in cases of violence against women after the worldwide lockdown in March 2020.

The thoughts that kept brewing in my mind now needed to be voiced. This led me to conduct a series of short videos called 'Things My Mother Didn't Teach Me'. These were short videos about a spectrum of observations made by me, and were driven purely from my personal experience. I received flak on social media: "Why is it only about mothers?"

The answer is simple. If you observe, nurturing is primarily done by mothers, and in this process, they pass their inhibitions, fears, and prejudices to their children. So, children grow up in a more progressive environment when taught about gender parity from childhood, and the impact on their lives and our society is significant. Women would become bolder, more confident, and begin loving themselves.

As a daughter and a mother, have the courage to speak up and say, "I have my rights. I have the right to express my sexuality, the right to my plate, I have the right to choose my life status, I have the right to speak up or stay silent; it is my choice. But I need not be told what is good or bad for me, every time. No one will speak up for me if I don't speak up."

If mothers don't teach their children the value of gender neutrality, we are losing the battle.

Self-care is the source of happiness and the right of every human being. So, we need to value ourselves. We need to appreciate women for standing up for themselves and acknowledging that they have the courage to speak up.

Self-expression is imperative not only to thrive but to live a fulfilled life. So, let's coexist and co-create a society where women express themselves, and are appreciated for their individualism.

The Author is not an expert in these topics but speaks from personal experience.

Foreword

I have been working in the area of gender balance and women's leadership for several years as a coach, facilitator, and writer. I know that there is a lot of work to be done. According to the latest research in the Global Gender Gap Report 2024, it will take 134 more years to reach gender parity. India's ranking in the Gender Gap Index is a pathetic 129 out of 142 countries. Though we have improved in the health indicators, we fare poorly in terms of economic and political participation.

While legislation and policies have helped, the most important change has to happen in the mindsets of both men and women who have been impacted by centuries of patriarchy. Mindset shifts lead to behavioural changes, and this shift has to start early on. Parents, especially mothers, have a crucial role to play in this area. Mothers who favour the sons over the daughters, mothers who collude with the father to enforce different boundaries for sons and daughters, and mothers who are hyper-anxious about having an unmarried daughter on their hands, send a message that girls are less than boys. How do we raise our sons and daughters so that they go on to become confident, respectful individuals?

This is what Linnet Dave explores in this book. I have known Linnet from the time when we both were trainers and consultants, and now our focus and interest are on women's rights and gender equality. As Linnet shares her stories and lived experiences of many women, we understand that women have unwittingly become torchbearers of patriarchy. I am able to see many examples of the four strategies I describe in my book "Powerful" - Deter, Diminish, Divide, and Decorate, that have been used to keep women from their power. The glorification of sacrifice and abnegation, the burden of being a perfect multitasker, and the pressure to bear the emotional load of the entire family, weaken women and erode their power. Linnet also shares tools, strategies, and ways to overcome the challenges, and move to a place of self-compassion and self-acceptance.

Linnet's voice comes from a place of personal lived experiences in a patriarchal system. It is an act of courage and vulnerability to share our stories. This is necessary. As each woman raises her voice and speaks to others, it empowers us as a collective.

I wish Linnet all the best for the book and hope it creates a spark in the readers that can light up the way to a more equitable society.

– Nirupama Subramaniam
Author of book "Powerful"

Chapter 1

Be Compassionate Towards Yourself

———————— ❈ ————————

"It is a matter of disdain that I don't get my rights.

I'm not making a comparison.

I'm simply asking for my rights as an individual."

Sasha simply hated her neighbour for being untidy.

"You know, my neighbour is like Pig-Pen; his house is filthy, and so is he."

"Why so?" questioned her friend, Vicky.

"He isn't married," she said.

"Well, is that a reason?" chuckled her friend.

 Sasha shirked.

"Yes, he has no wife to clear the mess. Who would clear the mess then?"

"So, would you clear all the mess at your home when you are married?"

Furious, irritated, and disgusted, "Never," she said.

As if she was Born to Clean up the Mess

"We've begun to raise daughters more like sons,
but few have the courage to raise our sons more
like our daughters."

-Gloria Steinem.

During our growing up years, we are told either directly or through subtler ways, that girls are easier than boys as they are vulnerable and can be instructed, while they meekly follow orders.

We are conditioned to be compassionate to others even if we suffer doing so. But we are never told that being compassionate towards self is also necessary. Self-love is natural, and we need not feel guilty about it.

No, I never thought I came first. Prioritising my health and self-care made me feel guilty. I was never told that asking for 'me time' or resting was my prerogative, and no one could snatch it away from me. I owe it to myself, no matter what people around me think about me.

Making that assertion never came to my mind. I kept compromising my well-being to ensure everyone around me was happy. Probably, then I would become worthy of all the praise and adulation, at the cost of my own being. What kind of martyrdom was this, which I imbibed and incidentally, I felt so proud about?

There were days when I would be totally exhausted, lacking sleep and rest, but after returning back home, it was expected that I clean the kitchen. Believe me, asking my husband to clean it up is asking for "too much". But why do we need someone else to assure us, "It is okay if you don't clean the kitchen. Instead, catch up on your sleep."

When was the last time we said, "Don't do it, woman. You deserve that rest?"

Instead, someone else in the family could do the cleaning and cooking while we rest. Sudha Murthy rightly shares her views about men helping with household chores in an article in The Times of India, 'Why Sudha Murthy feels men should be better at household work than women'.

"Boys should know better household work, actually much more cooking than girls. Reason being that if you want a wife who will work with you, who will bring home almost the same salary, then don't say 'my mother used to cook fantastic things.' Your mother was a housewife; she could do all those things."

When you expect your wife, who works as hard, to be like your mum, how do you expect the moment she comes home she should be like your mother? She comes home around 8 p.m.

Self-compassion is about:

Taking care of yourself.

Grabbing that much-needed rest and sleep. Loving yourself enough.

Believing you are precious.

Accepting that you owe it to yourself.

Realising that caring for yourself is not being selfish.

So, self-compassion should come naturally and not as a forced act. You should not be filled with guilt when you take care of yourself.

Because You are Worth It.

The origin of this tagline, 'I'm worth it', or rather a slogan, was inscribed by a 23-year-old woman in 1971 when the women's empowerment movement was gaining popularity. Most advertisements **objectified women** instead of empowering them. It was an age when men overpowered the advertising industry. Ilon Specht, a young copywriter, thought about breaking the norms.

She observed that women did things to be attractive to men. She wished women to be more assertive and contemporary so that it would benefit them. So, she created a commercial that established women having an identity beyond men in their lives, thus reiterating the fact that they are worth it.

A timeless slogan was penned by a young woman, encouraging women to recognise their own worth.

Despite these refreshing and reassuring slogans, it is true that women have been objectified, and we have been seen as an asset to be acquired and flaunted.

In fact, it becomes evident in the adage, '*Jar, joru aur jameen*' (wealth, woman, and land), which clearly identifies women as an asset. It states that wealth, woman, or land is the cause of all quarrels and malice in this world, thus objectifying women and reducing them to an asset that needs to be acquired.

Were We This Regressive In The Past?

In ancient India, women were treated with respect and dignity. During this period, there were women *rishis*, and they were held in high esteem. In royal households, women were respected; they even rendered a significant contribution to making decisions and administrative functions. They were made aware in all areas and played an important role in politics as well.

In the research paper, 'The saga of women's status in ancient Indian civilisation', Bhaswati Pal says that in the Early Vedic or the Rig Vedic Period (1500 BC–1000 BC), women had a respectable place in society. In the Dravidian culture, women participated in home, family, and socio-cultural activities. They engaged in war, archery, education, horse riding, public activities and gymnastics. They had the freedom to choose their male partners as well. Sculptures depict that in the early Vedic society, women enjoyed a higher status. They had equal opportunities to study the Vedas; in fact, women were seers and sages who wrote Vedic mantras as well.

Women enjoyed autonomy in family affairs and were considered Ardhangini (better half) and Sahadharmini (equal partner). Marriage was never done forcefully. They could select their life partners through Swayamwara. The remarriage of widows was socially acceptable. Women were also economically independent. They could participate in debates in public assemblies.

Special attention was rendered to women, and it was a matter of great priority that she was satisfied while having sex with her partner, as observed in *Vātsyāyana's Kāmasūtra*, which speaks about Rig Vedic sexual eroticism and emotional fulfillment in life.

But over the years, things changed drastically. Ironically, we had to fight for our rights. We women never had it easy.

It became an accepted fact that women would have to fight for their rights. Whether it's a fight for the right to vote, the right to education, the right to express themselves freely, etc. We had to ask for our rights while men got them on a platter. Inherently, that is what they deserved, and they should have it because they are men.

How Will All This Change?
Mothers Need To Demonstrate A Choice:

Mothers need to tell their children that women are entitled to their rights.

Make that choice to teach and ingrain in your children that women deserve self-compassion. Teach your children that women need to take care of themselves; they needn't compromise and sacrifice their well-being to take care of their families. Being tender, loving, and caring towards yourself is your right. Mothers should make that choice for you, and you should make it for the generations to come.

Through the years, being a part of a family that was rooted in patriarchy, made me suffocate. Let me share a personal experience that has been deeply ingrained in my mind. My brother and father are not on talking terms; they are estranged. Yet, he would do everything necessary for my brother as the man of the family.

On the other hand, I'm expected to be courteous and loving towards my father, who has been unfair and mean to me because I'm a daughter.

I'm expected to be loving. I'm expected to be forgiving.

I'm expected to be compassionate. I'm expected to be compromising.

I'm expected to sacrifice. I'm expected to multi-task.

Do I wish to end these expectations that are burdening me? Or do I wish to continue fulfilling these expectations?

This vicious cycle will end only when I decide that expectations towards myself are of prime importance.

***"To fall in love with yourself is the first
secret to happiness."***

- Robert Morley

Thus, it's about the choice you make.

The choice of protecting your own identity. The choice of protecting your interest.

The choice of loving yourself.

The choice of being answerable to yourself. The choice of taking care of yourself.

The choice of telling your posterity that you are worth it. But we are not making these choices.

My mother didn't teach me to make these choices. She didn't teach me to be compassionate to myself.

She didn't teach me that I come first and self-love is necessary.

There are some traits that women inherit from their mothers or rather learn from them and imbibe from their upbringing. They do not necessarily aid self-growth. In fact, they harm us and our self-esteem. Being compassionate is so necessary for every human. It is a gender-neutral virtue. But while growing women are told to be compassionate to others and always be kind towards others, even if it is at the cost of their happiness and emotional well-being.

Women blame themselves when something goes wrong, but we need to allow ourselves to be wrong at times. Let's give ourselves the leeway to be wrong, and not overdo things until the point of perfection. We are personified as embodiments of strength, probably to ask a lot more from us. It builds the premise to extract more from us, thus doing grave injustice to us.

Remember, you need to rest, so that you don't get emotionally drained. Have compassion for yourself. Why can't you grab those 15 minutes to comfort yourself, and not immediately begin doing housework as soon as you come back from the office? Allow your body to heal from pain, tiredness, and exhaustion. When you return home from work, you need to uncoil and rest like everyone else. Give yourself those precious moments of self-care.

We women have compassion, but it's outwardly, not inwardly. Showing compassion towards yourself is vital to healing and unburdening yourself of self-righteousness. While you hug your child, husband, mother, brother, or friend, hug yourselves and smile at yourselves to say, 'I'm totally worth it.'

When someone fails or is hurt, we women become their emotional cushion. Women love to be in this role. We are bred to be caregivers and told it is a virtue extremely vital for femininity.

Being compassionate towards yourself is forgiving yourself for failures and for making mistakes. It is about totally accepting yourself with all your flaws and not engaging in self-blame.

Self-compassion, as explained by Dr. Kristin Neff, is the act of being compassionate towards yourself even in testing times, through failures, or even after noticing that you don't like something about yourself.

We need to ask ourselves, "Are we ignoring our pain?" Or do we say, "At present, it is tough for me." We need to understand how to care for and comfort ourselves at the moment.

But let's not mix self-compassion with self-esteem and confidence. Dr. Neff says that self-compassion is different in many ways, though it might seem similar to self-esteem.

Self-esteem is about knowing your self-worth, perceived value, or how much you like yourself.

"Women, forget about all the criticism; it is going to be there.

Believe in what you are doing, and you will succeed."

- Kiran Mazumdar Shaw

But self-compassion is not about evaluating yourself. You are being kind to yourself even when you fail or do not perform well. In fact, everyone deserves compassion and understanding, not because one possesses certain traits or qualities that are laudable.

Let's accept that we deserve compassion and self-care too.

'Meta-Analysis of Gender Differences in Self-Compassion', a research paper penned by Lisa M. Yarnell, Rose E. Stafford, Kristin D. Neff, Erin D. Reilly, Marissa C. Knox, and Michael Mullarkey, mentions,

- Women prioritise others' needs over their own, as they are socialised with the norm of self-sacrifice. This affects their ability towards self-compassion (Baker-Miller, 1986; Raffaelli & Ontai, 2004; Ruble & Martin, 1998).

- Women are also self-critical and engage in more negative self-talk compared to men (DeVore, 2013; Leadbeater, Kuperminc, Blatt, & Hertzog, 1999).

- When your friend goes through a tough time, you would be compassionate, and you would be the same while you are going through a rough patch in your life. That is self- compassion.

You notice the suffering of others and empathize, so you do the same with yourself, offering understanding and kindness.

All said and done, we understand others and be kind and compassionate to others at the cost of hurting ourselves, and that is certainly not desirable.

I would like to give an example from my own life too. During the pandemic, we were all at home, and my husband suffered from COVID. He was quarantined, but gradually my son, in-laws, and I, tested positive. We all had to be at home. During those 15-20 days, I ensured everyone took proper medication, cooked food for them, and also continued my office work. My friend warned me that I needed to rest, but I was so involved in taking care of everyone that I completely neglected myself. Eventually, one day my body gave up, and I collapsed on the floor, unconscious for 40 minutes. How could I be so insensitive towards my health, rather ruthless towards myself?

That is how we do grave injustice towards ourselves in the bid to do everything for others.

If you try to please everyone, you will please no one. It is impossible to lead your life for others' happiness.

- Sudha Murthy

Today, I strongly believe that I need to be compassionate towards myself. Self-care and self-love are as important as loving somebody else. Keeping my own emotional tank full is important for a happy relationship. To be able to give love to others, I should be full of love towards myself too. I have learned this over a period of time, and now I take care of myself.

Raise yourself to be more compassionate towards yourself first.

Zia Mody rightly puts it:

"I always say that equality is defined on the dining table. How your siblings behave, how your parents treat your siblings, the level of confidence that you grow up with as a child - all of these go a long way in defining your journey. And so, it is not difficult to extrapolate."

"I was argumentative. I had a voice at the table, and of course, my parents, particularly my mother, pushed for me to get the best possible education.

Thus, it is vital that we bring up our children to believe inherently in gender equality."

From the book 'Fierce Self-Compassion' by Dr. Kristin Neff

Test Your Level of Self-Compassion

If you want to get a sense of how self-compassionate you are, you can fill out this brief version of the Self-Compassion Scale that is used in most self-compassion research.

Instructions

Please read each statement carefully before answering. To the left of each item, indicate: How often do you behave in the stated manner? Answer according to what really reflects your experience rather than what you think your experience should be.

For the first set of items, use the following scale from 1 (almost never) to 5 (almost always), or at some point in between:

_ I try to be understanding and patient towards those aspects of my personality I don't like.

_When something painful happens, I try to take a balanced view of the situation.

_ I try to see my failings as a part of the human condition.

_When I'm going through a very hard time, I give myself the care and tenderness I need.

__When something upsets me, I try to keep my emotions in balance.

_When I feel inadequate in some way, I try to remind myself that feelings of inadequacies are shared by most people.

For the next items, use a scale from 1 (almost always) to 5 (almost never), or some point in between. Notice that the scoring system has been reversed so that higher scores indicate lessened frequency:

__When I fail at something important to me, I become consumed by feelings of inadequacy.

When I'm feeling down, I tend to feel like most other people are probably happier than I am.

When I fail at something that's important to me, I tend to feel alone in my failure.

When I'm feeling down, I tend to obsess and fixate on everything that's wrong.

I'm disapproving and judgemental about my own flaws and inadequacies.

I'm intolerant and impatient towards those aspects of my personality that I don't like.

Total (sum of all 12 items) =   .

Mean self-compassion score (Total/12) =   .

In general, you can interpret a score ranging from 2.75 to 3.25 as average; below 2.75 as low, and above 3.25 as high.

Tasks:-

1. *Identify two ways of being self-compassionate. Incorporate them into your daily routine.*

2. *Note how you felt after being self-compassionate and the challenges you faced while doing so.*

Positive self-talk

While I'm still learning to live in the moment, I might fail or win. Either way, I understand that being perfect is not the purpose of life.

It is perfectly okay to be wrong; it is perfectly okay to be upset and angry at times.

I will not do things that make me unhappy just to please someone or be accepted, just because I love that person.

I will forgive myself even when I fail, and accept myself the way I am.

I love myself and accept myself through each moment of life, now and always.

Chapter 2

Don't Endure Sexual Abuse

**"Me being raped is not my fault.
I'm not going to be a victim. I will speak up!!"**

It had been days since Sasha hadn't visited the garden. A few days later her friend Vicky saw her sulking.

"Where have you been?" asked Vicky.

No answer, not a word.

Vicky looked worried and he queried.

"What's wrong? Why do you look hurt? Who is that? Tell me now. I can fix anything for you!"

Sasha told her friend, "I'm not supposed to speak about it. My mother told me so."

"Why?" shouted Vicky.

"Uncle touched me, and I hated it. But it's me who should never say a word, never ever dare."

Vicky hugged her, and Sasha knew it was different – this touch was out of love and not the same.

"Each time a woman stands up for herself without knowing it, without claiming it, she stands up for all women."

— Maya Angelou

As Bob Marley's song was playing in the background, "Get up, Stand up, Stand up for your right." Those words were blaring. The song that inspired many, now touched me the most. The song made me reminisce about all those occasions, where I was told not to stand up for my rights. On many occasions, I was told by my mother, to never speak about sexual abuse. She believed women should not revolt. Women should never speak against their husbands, brothers, or any male member. A typical patriarchal setup that represses women, and tells them to blanket the dark realities of life.

May it be Nirbhaya, Shakti Mills, Bengaluru's night of horror, or the Manipur rape case, women have been attacked horrendously. Justice comes late or probably never comes.

Isn't it true that we girls don't have it easy? The battle isn't over; we are still fighting many battles in our daily lives. One such intense fight that scars women for a lifetime, is not being able to fight against sexual abuse. In most cases, it is someone we trust the most, family members, or relatives who take advantage of the fact that they are trusted.

Even if we speak up, often it's neglected.

"Oh, it's okay. What's the big deal?"

Or else fear is instilled in us.

"No, never speak about it. Don't revolt."

Or we aren't trusted.

"How dare you accuse your uncle? For heaven's sake, he is family. He will never do anything like that."

Do we girls have to always keep quiet and never say a word?

Never revolt.

If we have been touched, in a manner we don't like, don't we have the right to speak up and say, "I hate it, please stop!"

Why Is It So Tough To Speak Up?

If we try to find out how many girls are being abused behind closed doors, we are never going to get an honest answer.

"In order to escape accountability for his crimes, the perpetrator does everything in his power to promote forgetting. If secrecy fails, the perpetrator attacks the credibility of his victim. If he cannot absolutely silence her, he tries to make sure no one listens."

- Judith Lewis Herman

From the book, 'Trauma and Recovery:

The Aftermath of Violence From Domestic Abuse to Political Terror.' by Judith Lewis Herman

Why Don't We Speak?

At crucial junctures of life, women are expected to keep quiet and shut up. Boisterous and outspoken women are shunned. All said and done, it's tough to speak about how disgusting it felt when you were touched in a wrong way. Something so intense churns within; it cannot be expressed in words. The scars remain forever, while the culprit goes scot-free, without even an iota of guilt or remorse.

"No amount of me trying to explain myself was doing any good. I didn't even know what was going on inside of me, so how could I have explained it to them?"

From the book, 'Debbie' by Sierra D. Waters.

Sexual abuse is difficult to speak about due to the stigma and shame attached to it. Young girls face it at school, in social circles, or sometimes at home too. They hesitate to speak, but even though they do choose to open up, family members might ask them not to utter a word about it, especially if it is a relative or a close friend.

While we raise our children, have we made them feel secure, safe, and protected?

If we tell them to never speak for themselves and stay mum, while someone touches them in a wrong manner, are we creating a safe world for them? We are just instilling a sense of insecurity and fear.

Where is this rooted?

Were women sexually abused in ancient times?

This adds fear, and shame gets attached, not to the act but about self, to the extent where the victim starts blaming herself and feels repulsive about her own body. Here, the victim feels guilty and shameful, adding fear, anxiety, and depression.

The society begins to blame the girl or woman facing sexual abuse, and is further abused when told to never speak about it. The first support system is our family, and if support fails to come from them, the damage is for a lifetime.

Women find it confusing to decipher the social norms that protect the perpetrator and blame the victim. Personal, societal, and legal challenges exist, that prevent us from disclosing the abuse and getting the help that we deserve.

Every woman knows the intention with which she is touched or looked at. She realises that she has been treated differently or abused. We are not taught to speak; rather, we are told to be quiet about it. Women need to realise they are the victim and there is no shame in voicing their disgust and anger. Let the perpetrator be known in public, because if you don't speak up, someone else might also suffer, and you will continue to suffer too.

The abuse might be a slight touch, or a verbal dialogue, might even be a word, but it is abuse, and you should have the courage to say it out loud.

The global fashion brand Elle, came up with a unique idea that gave voice to many women, to speak about the incidences of sexual abuse they experienced in their lives, and it was known as #MyFirstTime.

Women have shared such horrendous cases of sexual abuse like groping in public, touching of private parts in buses, pinching buttocks on a bus, molestation by a father's best friend's son, and many more such shameful incidents.

A survey conducted in 2019 by the Martha Farrell Foundation, revealed that over 58% of the population living in tier II towns believe:

Men have complete rights over their wives after marriage, and it is right for men to dictate to their wives.

88% said that a woman's happiness is all about nurturing her family.

The majority of the participants in the survey were aged between 13 and 15 years.

43% of the participants believe that women invite sexual harassment due to their dressing sense and their behaviour.

21% approve of husbands beating their wives in order to discipline them.

34% said that women should avoid travel jobs.

"India lodged an average of 86 rapes daily, 49 offences against women per hour in 2021: NCRB data," an article published in The Hindu mentions:

In the year 2021, India registered 31,677 rape cases, which adds up to an average of 86 daily.

Nearly 49 crime cases against women were lodged every hour in India, as per the latest government report on crime.

In 2020, rape cases were 28,046 as per the National Crime Records Bureau's (NCRB functions under the Ministry of Home Affairs) report called 'Crime In India 2021'.

Rape cases reported in 2021 in India were 65,025 in number.

The accused were known to the victim in 96.8 percent of the rape cases, according to the National Crime Records Bureau (NCRB) data.

What is even more alarming is that men don't realise the crime they are committing. In the book 'Why Men Rape: An Indian Undercover Investigation', a book by Tara Kaushal, is a documentation of an in-depth investigation, delving into the reasons for the increasing number of rapes in India. She has interviewed nine Indian men who have been involved in sexual violence and rape. These men come from different social strata, class, caste, religion, income, and region.

During these interviews, through her probing, alarming responses came her way. None of the nine perpetrators understood the meaning or the importance of consent from the female partner, while engaging in the act of sex. They didn't even respect them as individuals possessing their own distinct identity. One of them was a serial rapist who never accepted the idea of rape.

Our so-called "modern" society is not devoid of vulgarity and offensive acts inflicted on women. But were things the same during olden times?

Dr. R. Radha in her paper, 'Historical perspective of violence against women in India through various ages', published in 2019 in the Journal of Basic and Applied Research International, mentions that every human being is born free and deserves to enjoy this freedom. But women's freedom has been neglected in the name of honour, customs, social prestige, and family welfare.

In India, the status of women has been changing continuously over many years.

Dr R. Radha mentions,

"Women have been bound as mysterious creatures, as well as devoted mothers and self-sacrificing wives, during various periods of time, through which human civilisation has evolved from its primitive roots to an advanced scientific and technical culture."

Status of women changed due to many reasons like the marriage system, religion, education, and Purdah system. The Vedic period marked women getting equal status in society (Indra Kulshresthra, 1990:34). Rigveda discourages sexual violence, physical, and psychological violence against women.

Brishti Guha, in an article written for Times of India, says that the Rigveda mentions a rape and the victim called Ushas (Dawn), who then flees to a cave, was traumatised. Later, she is befriended by rishis who track her down to offer praise and support. Singers praise her radiance and lustre, trying to convince her to come out, and she does. Society did not judge Ushas; people offered support, boosted her morale, and helped her to overcome post-traumatic depression to navigate into a happy and normal life. The rape survivor was not stigmatised, and the child born out of rape wasn't looked down upon.

But over the years, the social status of women deteriorated with practices like the Devadasi system in the 7th century. It simply translates to 'Servant of God', and prepubescent women were married to God, just to be sexually exploited by the priests and upper-class men. The practice still prevails. In fact, they are not allowed to marry any man. This prevailed mostly in South India during the Chola, Chera, and Pandya dynasties.

> *"A Wife is half the man, the best of friends,*
> *The loot of the family and its perpetuity,*
> *The source of well-being... Wives are friends,*
> *in the wilderness."*
> *– Vatsyayana*

Research work done by Gurvinder Kalra and Dinesh Bhugra titled 'Sexual violence against women: Understanding cross-cultural intersections', mentions that sexual violence is due to unequal power equations between men and women, and it could be real or perceived. These perceptions are formed mostly due to cultural forces and values.

Cultures that are defined as feminist assign equal power to women and men. Sexual violence often occurs in societies that encourage the perception that men are superior and women are inferior.

Culture is a major factor in understanding sexual violence. United Nations mentions:

- Across the lifetime of women, 1 in 3 of them, i.e., around 736 million, go through physical or sexual violence by an intimate partner or from someone else other than the partner. These statistics have more or less remained the same over the past decade. This is surely a point of worry. It implies that there has been no change in the situation so far.

- Violence begins early. One in four women aged between 15 and 24 years, who have been in a relationship, have already faced violence from their intimate partner by the time they reach their mid-twenties.

- Globally, violence from intimate partners has by far been the most prevalent form of violence against women. It has affected 641 million women.

- 6% of women have reported sexual assault by someone other than their partner. However, one must understand that the stigma attached to reporting sexual abuse makes it tough for women to take legal action or report a case. Thus, the true figure must be significantly high.

- The truth is, that less than 40% of women who undergo sexual violence reach out for help of any kind. In most countries, with whatever data is available on this issue, among women who reach out for help, they usually look to their family and friends, but very few choose to report it to formal institutions like the police or health services.

- Less than 10 percent seek help from the police.

Why are we not speaking? Because there is no safe and secure environment where both men and women can thrive together. We tell our daughters to cover themselves properly because a certain type or style of dressing can provoke men, and result in sexual abuse or even rape.

Really, is it so? Women provoke and instigate men to rape them or sexually abuse them? Is it an invitation to be abused and raped? In fact, the way we dress is an expression of our personality. We have all the rights to express our individuality.

Why are we being punished for it?

Have we created a safe environment for our women? We have failed to raise men who respect women, and we have further failed by shutting our daughters up in revolt against the sexual abuse they face.

Khushbu, the famous South Indian actress, shared her experience of being sexually abused by her father from the age of eight, which opened up the conversation about rape and incest in the South Asian countries. She mentions that only at the age of 15, she had the courage to speak up against him. Till then, she suffered. These revelations about sexual abuse were shared at an event where school and university students were present. This created ripples in the country where rape and sexual harassment cases go unreported. Why? Because of the stigma attached to it and the fear of retribution.

"My mother has been through the most abusive marriage with a man who probably thought it was his birthright to beat up his wife, beat up his children, sexually abuse his only daughter."

"When my abuse started, I was just 8 years old, and I had the courage to speak against him when I was 15."

"One fear that stayed with me was that my mum may not believe me because I have seen her in that environment where there was 'kuch bhi hojaye mera pati devata hai' (no matter what happens, my husband is my God) mindset."

I was talking to my friend about how sexual abuse is prevalent in modern India in families, and I opened up about my story.

In fact, when I was studying in college, a relative visited our home and grabbed me at the entrance and kissed me. He was about to proceed further when I just pulled myself away from him and ran away like crazy. I shared this incident with my mother, hoping that she would understand and support me, but I was in for a big surprise.

My mother plainly said, "Shut up and don't talk about it."

I was violated and felt no longer safe in my own home. In fact, he kept coming home when my parents weren't around. Women across various cultures and economic strata face this at home and are told to shut up.

My friend had an even more traumatic experience that she shared with me.

"Lin, I was raped in my childhood. My maternal uncle used to call me to a temple under the pretext of conducting Puja and raped me every single day for six years. After I became an adolescent, he told me to send my younger sister to him. I was petrified but denied. So, he asked me to keep coming to him, and this continued until I was 20 years old. Lin, I never got my menses until the age of 20. My parents took me to a counsellor to whom I opened up.

My childhood has been stolen from me, and my parents have been in a state of shock after knowing what my uncle had been doing. I'm sure in many Indian homes this is what happens, and we never speak up. I wish I had screamed, I wish I had the courage to scream loud until the world knows about this horrendous act. It is my body, and I should protect it."

Sexual abuse is not gender- or age-specific.

In Thane, a 27-year-old bus attendant allegedly molested six girls and two boys. This incident occurred in the evening when the children were returning from an excursion. The 27-year-old attendant made the children sit on his lap to touch his private parts while he was distributing snacks. The children had been taught to identify good touch and bad touch. These children shared this incident with their parents. The police arrested the abuser. Thankfully, hundreds of parents supported the parents of the molested children. Parents stood outside the entrance of the school, and no parents sent their children to school until the principal was terminated. The principal and CEO of the school were suspended from their services until an internal enquiry completed.

Things are changing, and children are now being educated about abusive behaviour. They do speak about it, express, and revolt.

When Will These Shameful Acts Stop?

Only when you choose to speak up and instil the courage among your children to speak up.

Tasks:

1. Have you ever faced any kind of sexual abuse? Did you choose to report it?

2. Talk to a close friend or relative if they have faced any kind of abuse. Share your experience as well.

Positive self-talk

A Promise to Myself:

Whenever I face any kind of sexual violence or abuse, I will speak about it.

In such a case, I won't feel guilty or shameful.

When I am touched in a wrong manner, I will revolt and speak up.

Openly speaking about my experience is my right and not a matter of shame.

I'm powerful enough to fight it out, and I need not fear anything at all.

I need no pity; the aim is to punish the perpetrator so that he is not left scot-free to keep repeating the act.

I'm special and no one can touch me wrongly, say anything abusive, or hurt me in any way.

Chapter 3

Reciprocity

"She is supposed to sacrifice her happiness for the family. That is her duty!"

Both Sasha and Vicky were playing with other kids in the garden.

Vicky had a bad fall, and he was in pain.

Sasha ran to comfort him.

Vicky was touched and he hugged her, "You are so lovely. Thanks!"

Sasha was flushed with emotions. "A few days back, I was sad, and you were there for me. You are lovely too."

Thus, they bonded well and built the edifice of a stronger friendship.

"Women support their men when they're building companies and careers; men must also support their women."

- Sudha Murty

A couple of days back, I saw a touching movie called *Thappad*, which raised innumerable questions in my mind. The movie is about Amrita, the protagonist, whose life is perfect until her husband slaps her at a party. That one slap is enough for her to take an audit of her relationship. In fact, she starts realizing she has no say in the relationship, since she is working endlessly to keep her husband happy, while he is totally unacknowledging. Amrita cooks breakfast, cleans and decorates the house, takes care of her son and mother-in-law also; when her husband is angry, she is there to take a hit from him at a party in front of everyone. All she does is give in the relationship at the cost of her self-respect. He believes he did no wrong; he says it's a deal. He works to make money, and she is there to keep him happy. He is self-obsessed and always involved in his professional life, and for him, Amrita exists only to take care of him and his family.

She refuses to forgive him for slapping her and asks for a divorce. The general perspective is that it's just a slap. But no, for her, it's her respect and her individuality that have been questioned. Her husband sees no point in her asking for a divorce. In fact, he is absolutely brutish and unapologetic. Even when he does apologise, it is out of helplessness – accepting the fact that he cannot run the house single-handedly.

She gets a divorce and begins a new life.

Every relationship on the face of this earth is symbiotic. Not expecting anything out of a relationship isn't practical. Relationships thrive on reciprocity, not on sacrifice.

My mother has always been a sacrificing woman. She has never spoken for herself, her well-being, health, or rights, just about anything. She has suffered in silence. She has given herself completely in her relationship as a wife and a mother. But my father has never acknowledged her sacrifice. In fact, he always believed, 'She is supposed to do that; it's her duty'. My mother had duties to perform but was not granted any rights.

She was never cared for, never loved, never nurtured, never admired, never, ever. We are told, "Never have any expectations from your husbands." Does that mean they are so unworthy that we cannot expect anything from them?

For the homogeneously intelligent, powerful, and empathetic woman that Sudha Murthy is, she has some great thoughts on relationships that I adore.

"I don't control him; similarly, he doesn't control me. We respect each other's passion; we respect each other's space. And still, you can be different and still be together. Like I always say – opposite poles attract each other!"

"Men can do certain things well, and women do other things. Men and women are complementary to each other. One need not prove one's strength."

- Sudha Murty

Men and women are different from each other, yet they are beautiful in their own way. We need not compare nor compete. We need to respect our individuality and not consider anyone inferior.

The challenge here is in the regressive approach towards women we have many a times, the lack of self-reflection and self-love that women have towards themselves. Has anyone ever indicated to us that we need not admire ourselves and always depend on someone else to love us? If we don't care about ourselves, no one will. And the day a woman begins to appreciate her inner beauty and power, she will never need a relationship that doesn't involve reciprocity. All relationships that carry no amount of respect for her will perish at the hands of her self-belief.

So as women have been supportive of their life partners' passions, careers, and ambitions, a man too needs to reciprocate by being supportive of his wife.

I have seen my mother working endlessly in the kitchen without any rest. Forget about being praised, she was never acknowledged for all the housework she did, the selfless love and care she had for her husband and children.

I strongly feel it's about two things:

- Low self-esteem

- Extreme conditioning.

We should never compromise our self-esteem. But women are conditioned to believe that we should expect nothing in return for everything we do for our family.

What is a woman going through while she carries a volcano within her and never says a word? No one knows, and no one cares, as she suffers silently in her relationships.

Never become a martyr and kill yourself by compromising on your self-respect – ask for what you need out of a relationship. All relationships are two-way traffic. A relationship has to be healthy emotionally as that is the most critical factor in a committed relationship, irrespective of whether it's romantic or otherwise.

Love and support cannot be given by a single person. Every healthy relationship is about giving and receiving energy; it's a mutual exchange that holds the connection and bond together. But if there is a lack of reciprocity, one partner becomes a constant giver, while the other constantly receives. This exhausts the giver, leading to sheer frustration.

Peggy Hinders, a professional counsellor, says that open communication is at the core of a healthy relationship. Actively listening helps to acknowledge your presence and acceptance in the opposite person's life. She says one has to remember to take it. Everyone needs support at some point, so seek it.

> ***Avoid a non-reciprocal situation by taking, in addition to giving. Healthy interdependence is important in a relationship.***
>
> ***Peggy Hinders***

Nurture your relationship:

So, asking for what you need in a relationship is not an act of selfishness, but it is the only way you will keep the relationship thriving. Nurturing the relationship is important, and it goes both ways.

> ***We've got this gift of love, but love is like a precious plant. You can't just accept it and leave it in the cupboard or just think it's going to get on by itself. You've got to keep watering it. You've got to really look after it and nurture it.***
>
> ***— John Lennon***

Are you the giver in your relationship? Then you need to start asking for reciprocity.

"I need you to be around when I go to the doctor."

"Today, I'm totally exhausted. I can't clean the table. I want you to clean the table today."

"Can you make it to the parent-teacher meeting today? I'm totally tied up."

A woman should demand and say, "You take some part of the stress."

Why Do We Need To Ask For It?

Simply because most of the time your partner will not be able to identify that he or she is not nurturing the relationship by reciprocating, and also because what Napoleon Hill says is right.

"There is no such thing as something for nothing."

— Napoleon Hill

How can we be told and made to believe that we should not expect anything from a relationship? It is practically impossible not to expect. The act of accepting love, affection, and care, inherently means, in a relationship, that you accept to give (reciprocate) as well.

"Get me lunch." "Clean the table." "Get me my clothes."

"Why is the house so dirty?"

These sound like orders, not requests. If these instructions are being given constantly by one person in a relationship, while the other person just does these chores single-handedly, then you surely need to rethink the values on which the relationship is built.

Nothing can mar a relationship more than a lack of reciprocity.

Stop chasing!!

Stop chasing a person who doesn't reciprocate. If you put in all the efforts, yet the person refuses to understand and acknowledge your efforts in the relationship, then you need to stop chasing for his/her attention.

How is reciprocity rooted in human behaviour?

Seline Shenoy, an author, podcaster, and blogger, says that reciprocity is rooted deeply in our psychology. It is at the core of our social interactions and is vital to maintaining social order and cooperation among people. The psychological base of reciprocity is called the 'norm of reciprocity', which states that people feel obliged to return favours that they receive. This norm is experienced across cultures. It connects us to our humanness since it is based on our desire to maintain social harmony and fairness in society. When one person engages in a selfless activity, it sparks a sense of indebtedness in the receiver, and this results in reciprocity.

Democritus (fourth century BC) advised,

"Accept favours in the foreknowledge that you will have to give a greater return for them."

It is a grave injustice to the person who only becomes a giver.

So why do we forget in a love or marital relationship that you have to return that favour? In fact, if you ask for a favour in return, it is not being selfish. It is asking for reciprocity, and that is the basis of a human relationship. If you are well aware that your relationship needs to flourish, then you would surely do something for your partner. Isn't it?

My mother probably never realised that she could ask for favours from her relatives while they enjoyed all the festive sweets, she slogged alone in the kitchen to cook them. All she received from them was empty praise, but no one walked into the kitchen to extend a helping hand.

If you care for and respect your partner, you will surely know,

What matters to that person?

What hurts the person?

What makes that person happy?

Rather than just blatantly ordering and demanding favours, you will acknowledge her presence and start noticing her closely.

Anne Ream, Professional Counsellor and Marriage and Family Therapist, says,

For this, both partners have to accept responsibility. There is always an interdependence in a healthy relationship.

One person cannot take all the blame in a relationship, nor can one person do all the tasks. One needs to accept responsibility for creating a reciprocal relationship, and it also takes a high degree of emotional maturity, awareness, time, and personal work to develop.

Respect in a relationship should be reciprocal. Each person has to be respected, and you need to identify when you feel disrespected. You have to respect each other's ideas, belief systems, rights, intelligence, and value systems. Love won't grow if there is no respect.

It is deeply painful to see how often men disregard and disrespect their wives.

In our modern times, we have compromised on a woman's self-respect despite being educated, well-read, civilised, and cultured.

Things were never the same in ancient times.

This is how ancient Vedic culture viewed the partnership of Husband and Wife:

The Sanskrit term used by the husband for the wife was

Pathni (the one who leads the husband through life).

Dharmapathni (the one who guides the husband in dharma) and *Sahadharmacharini* (one who moves with the husband on the path of dharma: righteousness and duty).

In Rig Veda (10.85), the marriage hymn states that the daughter-in-law should be treated as a Queen, *sāmrajni*, by all the family members, especially the mother-in-law, husband, and father-in-law.

Source: https://vedah.com/ (Article: Women Sages of Rishikas)

A woman is referred to as:

Aditi, because she is not dependent (Nirukta, 4/22). *Aghnyā*, for she is not to be hurt (Yajur Veda 8/43). Dhruvā, for she is firm (Yajur Veda 11/64).

Havya, because she is worthy of invocation (Yajur Veda 8/43).

Idā, for she is worshipable (Yajur Veda 8/43).

Kāmyā, because she is lovable (Yajur Veda 8/43).

Menā, because she deserves respect (Nirukta 3/21/2).

Sarasvati, since she is scholarly (Yajur Veda 20/84).

Simhī, since she is courageous (Yajur Veda 5/12).

Sivā, for she is benevolent (Atharvar Veda 14/1/64)

Yoṣhā, because she is intermingled with man, she is not separate (Nirukta 3/15/1)

(Source : https://vedicheritage.gov.in/ pdf/Persona_of_Women_in_Veda.pdf)

So, when you think about your relationship with your partner, reflect on these three types of reciprocity:

(Source: Human Relations Area Files. Reciprocity & Exchange: The Kula Ring - **Francine Barone, Human Relations Area Files at Yale University by Dr. Francine Barone)**

Balanced reciprocity:

It is a situational act of favour. Like when you extend a favour and expect something specific in return out of your act of giving. Like, if you gift a birthday present, expecting something in return on your birthday.

Generalised reciprocity:

You give or extend a favour without expecting anything specific in return besides just goodwill. This is based on mutual respect and connection between two individuals. This kind of reciprocity is common between two people who love and trust each other – family members, friends, or couples.

Negative reciprocity –

This is never expected out of a healthy relationship – when you give less and receive a lot more in return.

So, you have to gauge where your relationship fits.

Let me share with you a beautiful example of reciprocity.

'*Sawubona*', a Zulu greeting that is translated as 'I see you'. It is a greeting that implies more than politeness; it is about recognising the worth and dignity of every person. It means that "We see you; me and my ancestors, see you and your ancestors, all that has brought you here – now to the present, this moment, in the physical form. We see all of who you are. We are open to all the perfection that has been created as you. We see who you truly are."

To '*Sawubona*', you reply back as '*Sikhona*' – "I'm here to be seen. I commit to showing up as my authentic self. I'm fully present here to share myself with you, as I am."

(Source: Loom International)

Task

Find out if you have a reciprocating relationship

1. Do you carefully and actively listen to your partner when he or she speaks?

2. Do you help your partner with household chores?

3. How often do you notice your partner being tired, worried, or a bit disturbed?

4. Do you speak out to your partner about what worries you and her?

5. How often do you both spend time nurturing each other's hobbies?

6. Have you spoken about your values, belief system, and passions?

7. Do you listen to each other's ideas and thoughts on various family matters, or do you end up fighting?

8. How often do you go on holidays?

9. Have you clearly communicated your expectations with each other?

10. Does your partner feel he/she is giving too much to the relationship compared to the other?

If the answer to most of the questions is 'yes', you are in a reciprocal relationship. But you can become more reciprocal by converting 'no' into 'yes' by working on your relationship.

Positive Self-talk

I will speak my mind and ask for favours. I will always do things that I love doing.

Actively listening to my partner is my responsibility.

Asking for help is okay in a relationship.

I will share the responsibilities with my partner.

Life is beautiful, and sacrifice cannot be one-sided to keep it that way.

I will always remember,

"Love is not self-sacrifice, but the most profound assertion of your own needs and values. It is for your own happiness that you need the person you love." - Ayn Rand.

Chapter 4

Walk Upright

Vicky seemed to be observing Sasha rather closely today.

He was silent, didn't know how to say it.

One of his friends asked him, "Vicky, what is it? Why are you looking like that at her?"

"Just like that – I was wondering why she was stooping low with her shoulders. She never does that."

Sasha overheard the conversation. "My mum said so – as girls, we are not supposed to sit upright. I don't know why she said so. But my back hurts now."

Vicky just held her shoulder and made her sit straight. "You look awesome like that – just the way it should be for everyone."

"It took me quite a long time to develop a voice, and now that I have it, I am not going to be silent."
– Madeleine Albright

A note to myself:

The way I express myself is my personality – you don't like it? Still, the core of me won't change.

I will bloom and flourish as I accept myself.

You can't dictate my being, nor can you lead me.

You can question, argue, and debate – but you can't set the norms for my life.

I live by my rules!

I lead my path and thrive on my own. I radiate my inner light.

I'm beautiful and love myself totally as I am!

It was Vaishali's birthday, and we were all jamming at her home.

It was pleasant in Mumbai since it had been raining for a while now. Vaishali was quiet.

"Hey, what's up with you? *Kyu gumsum ho* (why are you so silent)?" I asked her.

"Nothing, babe. A boy came over to see me yesterday – a proposal for marriage, I mean. Nothing like a formal meeting. We spoke at length about our lives and future plans. Everything seemed to be proceeding just fine, and I was about to call him over once again for lunch this time, when he said something totally unimaginable."

"I love women who are plump. You would look great if you put on weight. You know what I mean to say na, Vaishali."

I just smiled. To which he continued, "You know, busty women look sexy!"

That was it, I lost my mind!

Well, I said to myself, "Did I ask you to go to the gym and pump up a bit as I love well-built guys? Did I ask you to show off how you look?"

We all started fooling over this stupid comment and said, "Then you should have asked him to show his assets as well."

The room then filled with laughter when Vaishali started sharing some rave comments her neighbour passed on to her, "Vaishali, why do you walk upright? Your breasts stick out. You should stoop a bit lower on your shoulders and walk. Why don't you get married and have children? Women are incomplete until they have children. Who is this guy who came home – is he your boyfriend?" Blah, blah, blah… endless comments to which I say just one thing, "I'm happy with the way things are in my life. Don't bother!!"

One of my friends who was part of the jamming group broke into a song by Lesley Gore:

"You Don't Own Me

You don't own me

I'm not just one of your many toys

You don't own me

Don't say I can't go with other boys

And don't tell me what to do

Don't tell me what to say

And please, when I go out with you

Don't put me on display cause

You don't own me

Don't try to change me in any way

You don't own me

Don't tie me down cause I'd never stay

I don't tell you what to say

I don't tell you what to do

So just let me be myself

That's all I ask of you

I'm young and I love to be young

I'm free, and I love to be free

To live my life the way I want

To say and do whatever I please

And don't tell you what to do

Oh, don't tell me what to say

And please, when I go out with you

Don't put me on display

I don't tell you what to say

Oh, don't tell me what to do

So just let me be myself

That's all I ask of you

I'm young and I love to be young

I'm free, and I love to be free"

As the song started fading, in the middle of nowhere, Shilpa burst into tears. We were all confused. After consoling her and calming her down, she opened up,

"I left my 6-month-old daughter at home crying as she was inconsolable yesterday. I didn't wish to go to the office, but I had an urgent assignment. When I reached the office, my boss blasted me for walking in late. I just continued working until it was lunchtime. I was totally exhausted and looked depressed. My Boss saw my sullen mood and simply commented, 'Oh! You look tired, must be the hormones!'"

I was flabbergasted and uncontrollably shaky. I excused myself and burst out into tears in the washroom.

Why does it have to be only the hormones? After pregnancy, there has been a major shift in my body; it has transformed – it has changed completely. Don't they understand? It's not always hormones.

We were all silent and Rekha began strumming the guitar and sang, '*O Ri Chiraiya*', (written by Swanand Kirkire), a tribute to women's struggle.

The song played havoc in our minds, and I burst out saying, "Over and above all that I do, I cannot go to the temple when I have periods, as I'm supposed to be impure. Having my menses is so natural, and I'm blatantly denied permission? Women are worshipped in the form of Durga Maa, Kaali Maa … but when it comes to giving our rights, no one wishes to express the grave injustice done to us."

Sheila began to laugh, "C'mon, you know na how guys look at me since I chose not to marry and stay single. They call me a feminist in the most derogatory manner, hahaha…" She rolled into laughter. "Maybe they are jealous that I live a free life and have the courage to make my own decisions. They are jealous!"

She burst into laughter, yet again, and we all did.

She continued, "You know our fashion industry, the gyms that we visit, the weight loss advertisements we see are all focused on women. A woman's body is on display to attract more customers. Are we here for a display?"

I recently read an article written by Saumya Kalia titled as 'Indian Women Hold Only 10% of Directing, Writing Positions in Films and TV: Report' published on Swaddle in 2022, which mentions:

"In 2021, Indian women held almost 10% of industry positions such as editing, directing, writing, designing, and cinematography — in films and series streamed online. On-screen, this means women's stories are disembodied, told by people holding structural privilege, and told in a way that objectifies and stereotypes lived realities."

She continues by sharing a report done by O Womaniya! that examines 150 films released in theatres, including films and TV series, in 2021, across eight languages (Hindi, Tamil, Telugu, Malayalam, Kannada, Punjabi, Bengali, and Gujarati).

Out of the other figures, a key one is that of the 56 theatrical films surveyed in 2021, none of them had a woman Director or Editor. This is aligned with the cultural myth that women cannot survive in fast-paced environments, and women cannot handle pressure. Most Directors and industry professionals are male, so they most likely hire men as Dame Heather Rabbats, Chair of Time's Up UK, says that we tend to hire people of our own image.

But, I do feel sometimes, that women shown in most movies are a reflection of what the male director or writer has chosen to show – a male perspective.

I shared my view, too, "True, I totally agree with you, Sheila. You know I visited the Amer Fort in Rajasthan. The guide there prided on something that I felt was totally unjust to the Queens. In olden times when the queen was all decked up with exquisite clothes and jewellery, she had to depend on a wheelchair to move around due to the weight of the clothes and jewellery. Imagine how her body posture must have changed due to the weight. It must have been so uncomfortable and painful. Cruel, isn't it? But it was a matter of pride and tradition for the Royal Family."

Joanna (whose passion is poetry) wished to read a poem that she wrote while listening to our discussion. We were all ears.

I'm beautiful

My body is not the weight I carry.

Nor the remarks you make about it.

The inner radiance – is my beauty.

Thoughts, ideas, and views encompass my character.

A part of me that you shun,

And choose not to see.

Are all me - I'm beautiful!!

Not just a part or the flesh,

That you choose to see. I don't wish to hide.

In the blanket of traditions.

Falsely implicated to subdue

Never allow me to make a mark.

You blanket your insecurities.

With rave comments

Restricting me now is not possible.

I'm beautiful as I am,

As you are.

Not just a part

But whole of you!!

Task:

Observe, observe, and observe. Listen, listen, and listen.

Often, someone says something about the way you speak and behave.

Or the way you walk or dress.

A lot gets spoken about your life decisions – About not marrying and not having children. Bringing up your children –

Teaching them and nurturing them.

You don't like it.

But you don't object!

Try speaking out and expressing your emotions.

May it be in the family, among friends, or in the office. Speak out.

If you can't speak out, try writing about what stops you from expressing yourself.

What was said to you? Why didn't you like it?

What was your response, and why?

Positive self-talk

I will be full of self-confidence. I love myself as I am.

The innumerable questions that the world asks - I will face them all with confidence.

Moreover, I will not answer any.

Today, I'm going to smile and be happy. And celebrate my being.

I will shed –

All the stress and worry about being perfect. And will consider my happiness and health of prime importance.

I will take care of myself.

Stand up for my choices confidently.

Chapter 5

It's Your Choice to be Single, Not have Kids, or be a Professional

"A woman becomes complete only after bearing a child?"

Vicky looked puzzled as he said,

"My sister and her friends say they never want to marry.

Mum wishes she had never married."

"I overheard my mum saying that to a friend!"

"What is marriage all about?" asked his friend.

Sasha ran to Vicky and said, "It's all about love, I think!"

"Is it so beautiful, my friend?" asked Vicky.

Sasha flapped her hands and said, "Don't know. I cannot understand what they say."

"Nothing is more difficult, and therefore more precious, than to be able to decide."
- Napoleon Bonaparte

Being married and having kids in India is a great accomplishment, but without it, you are unsuccessful and incomplete. You know the feeling when you attend a wedding and while everyone is exchanging pleasantries, someone just pops out of nowhere to make you feel awkward, "When are you getting married? You are so pretty, so what is stopping you?"

As if being pretty or beautiful is an endorsement for marriage. At a time when you are truly enjoying your singlehood and have no intentions to start living with someone, or probably just had a break-up, or whatever the reasons to be single are, this question becomes totally irrelevant. Why is being single such a matter of discussion?

In fact, the statement, "I don't wish to get married," comes as a shocker to most people in India. You will be surprised that women in India are choosing to stay single.

According to a recent study conducted by Bumble in 2023 (an article published in News18, "Consciously Single' Dating Trend Shows How More Women Are Comfortable Being Single"), revealed that 39% of people in India feel pressurized by their families to participate in traditional matchmaking during the wedding season. Times have changed, and youngsters don't wish to participate in these traditional methods of matchmaking. They make their own choices, and that isn't bold. It simply means you know yourself better to be able to make that independent choice.

"Feminism isn't about making women stronger.
Women are already strong; it's about changing the
way the world perceives that strength."
– G.D. Anderson

Being single gives an opportunity to focus on self-growth, discover yourself better, and understand what makes you happy. Now, women really don't want to settle for less and are clear about what they need in their lives. They wish for someone who complements them, triggers happiness, and gives a deeper meaning to their lives. I feel it's your life, so you make the call — not someone else. Above all, no one should dig deeper into your reasons for being single because that is your personal space that cannot be hijacked by anyone.

Samarpita Samaddar, India Communications Director at Bumble, shares, "In India, during the wedding season, if you are single, people will begin querying about your single life and judging you. In fact, women also feel anxious about attending such functions since they are bombarded with these questions. These functions become a source of tension and anxiety."

An article in Pune Mirror, 'Consciously single and happy' (published in 2023), mentions that according to the Bumble study, 33% of unmarried Indians who were part of the survey said that they feel forced to enter a committed long-term relationship.

Also, Indians now give more importance to togetherness — people feel evaluated on the basis of being single due to single-shaming. People make unnecessary inquiries about how they date. The article further shares that the concept of single-shaming implies that being single is just a temporary situation and should be tackled rapidly; this thought is ingrained in the present popular culture and the Indian societal expectations.

Another concept of 'Consciously single' is becoming popular among Indians. Women are consciously choosing to stay single and not compromising on their preferences. They are being specific about their choices regarding who and how they wish to date.

It is a fact that according to the recent study by the Bumble app, 81% of women respondents in India felt more comfortable being unmarried and living alone. While 63% say they won't compromise on their requirements, preferences, and needs. 83% of women say they feel content to wait until they find the right person in their lives.

The study further states that women are in control of who and how they wish to date and what is of prime importance to them. This shift is so interesting that I feel totally excited listening to the fact that Indian women are in control. They are ready to wait for something more deserving, not getting too worried about rushing into marriage due to age.

No matter what choice a woman makes, it becomes a subject of discussion. A woman chooses not to marry, have a unique career, not have a career, or not have children. No matter what she chooses, she becomes answerable to a hell of a lot of people. Well, it is her life and her body.

She has the right, will, intelligence, and insight to choose for herself.

> ***"No woman should be told she can't make decisions about her own body. When women's rights are under attack, we fight back."***
>
> ***- Kamala Harris***

When we choose to have a career, a truly ambitious one, we are told to tone down a bit. They say that men get scared of ambitious women, so if one needs to live with a man, she needs to work less and adjust to her husband's schedule, and conclusively be less ambitious.

Having a career is absolutely a woman's choice, and at least her family should respect and support her decision. But the so-called guardians of society have time and again asked women to slow down a bit and compromise on their work timings.

Peter McGraw, Bachelors in Behavioural Economics, and Business School Professor, talks to Sreemoyee Piu Kundu – excerpts from the podcast.

Sreemoyee Piu Kundu, Author and an Advocate, was delivering a keynote lecture at CNBC Television. She shared with the audience that 39% of the Indian female population is now single. 21% of about 12 million women are single mothers.

20% to 21% of households are managed and run by solo primary breadwinners. Here she clarified that a single mother and a primary breadwinner, can be an unmarried daughter or a widowed daughter. After she delivered the keynote, heads of big organisations, decked in suits and ties, came up to her and said that they could not believe there are so many single women. She replied that she could not believe their response because in the Indian corporate world, about 30% to 50% of the workforce is single.

"This is a country where marriage and motherhood
are considered the holy grail of womanhood.
This is a country where as soon as a daughter is born,
we still have very high rates of female foeticide.
When the daughter is born, if she is allowed to see the
light of day, may I say that with a lot of shame about

my country? Immediately, she is labelled as Paraya Dhan, which means another's property."

– Sreemoyee Piu Kundu

When a woman decides not to have children, it comes with a lot of opposition. Not having children means the woman is selfish. She is either too ambitious, doesn't want to put her body through all the trouble, or she is heartless.

Not necessarily, marriage and motherhood are her only prime responsibilities in society. Are they?

Let's recheck with most women who have children – are they truly happy after being mothers? If they end up saying 'no', they will face harsh remarks. Why is a woman compelled to be a mother? In our society, we are raised to believe that getting married and having children is compulsory and it's what we are born to do.

"Women are incomplete without having children," this truly is a regressive statement.

The Hindustan Times' big story, 'Mind the Gap', penned by Namita Bhandare, mentioned,

> ***"The role of women as mothers from religious literature to popular culture is so ubiquitous that it makes you wonder if women actually have an authentic choice in the matter,"***

> ***"We are a pro-natalist culture where, as South Asians, we imagine children as the emotional pivot of our lives."***

- *Amrita Nandy, author of 'Motherhood and Choice:*
Uncommon Mothers, Childfree Women',
Childless Women.

Can't she choose not to have children? That doesn't necessarily imply that she wishes to enjoy her life. She might have other priorities. And even if she wishes to enjoy life, she is not wrong, since that is her personal choice.

"That, since day one, she's already had everything
she needs within herself. It's the world that convinced
her she did not."

– Rupi Kaur

Decisions regarding financial matters:

Here, I'm referring to the article titled, '51% of women in India prefer low-risk financial instruments; only 7% invest in stocks: Survey', in The Economic Times published in January 2024.

47% of women make independent financial decisions, while 51% prefer low-risk instruments, according to the report.

They mention an interesting study about Indian women. It says that 47% of women take financial decisions on their own, and this reflects the changing picture, where it reflects the changing momentum in women's financial independence. While 65% of women aged over 45 years, independently arrive at financial decisions, compared to 41% aged 25 to 35 years, as revealed by the latest study by CRISIL and DBS Bank India.

Today, women are not silent pillars for the family. They actively participate in decision-making. Based on the National Family Health Survey, urban women's participation in key household decisions increased to 91% in 2019-20 from just 49% in 2005-06.

47% of women take advice and information from family members when they need to make financial decisions since they value the trust and shared experience from kinship.

While on the other hand, 27% take a professional approach, taking advice from professional advisers and Chartered Accountants. However, this number is as low as 5% in Chennai and Coimbatore, where 70% of women seek family opinions when deciding on their finances, compared to the Indian average of 47%.

An article published in the Economic Times in March 2024 titled 'Financial Independence: How women are increasingly taking financial decisions' mentions that today, women are taking charge of their financial independence by venturing out of their conventional roles and redefining societal expectations. This change is helping women to attain financial security and stability. Women no longer just depend on their spouses for financial decisions.

Why Should Society Dictate A Woman's Life?

Why can't women stand up and speak for themselves? Why Can't Women Make Their Life Choices?

Why are we answerable to anyone about what we do with our lives?

You fear chaos in society if we make our own choice? Then – how come men get away with doing what they wish and never answer to anyone. Does that not lead to chaos?

***"If one man can destroy everything,
why can't one girl change it?"***

***– Malala Yousafzai, '
I Am Malala: The Story of the Girl Who Stood Up for
Education and was Shot by the Taliban'.***

This task can be simple yet complex.

Task 1

Write your thoughts about having children by being truly honest with yourself.

Share it with your family and journal their responses as well.

The key is being honest – irrespective of the fact that you are married, dating, or single.

Task 2

Also, write 5 of your choices that you wish to make in your life and ask yourself if you can make these choices without asking anyone or worrying about anyone else.

Positive self-talk.

I'm independent to make my own choice.

All the choices made by me are a result of all the experiences I go through and the wisdom I carry.

Let me not explain why I made a choice.

My life is a beautiful gift, and I wish to live it by making my own choices.

I might share a few of my choices with you and confide in you. That too is my choice!

My life is a result of my choices, and I'm happy with them.

Chapter 6

Stop Playing Victim

"What can I do without any support?
I'm alone and helpless."

Vicky consoled Sasha, "Don't cry. It's okay. You will score well in the next exam."

But Sasha continued crying.

Vicky shrugged his shoulders and retorted, "Tears are a woman's biggest weapon."

Sasha was all puzzled and queried, "What... what does that mean?"

"Don't know, my dad says that often to mum."

"A country like India has a lot of potential. I end with the hope that we will build on that. My life is my message: nothing is impossible."
— M.C. Mary Kom, Unbreakable

Tears are the biggest weapon of women. Time and again, we've heard this, and it's exhausting to repeatedly hear this statement. Though it is so cliché, it reflects the 'victim mentality' that women carry, and moreover, it shows that shedding tears is the only weapon we have in our armour. So, are tears that powerful? That is not true.

We are not victims, nor are we helpless. We have some unique strengths; thus, we have equal rights. When we glorify this victim mentality, showcasing it as a powerful weapon, the more we start believing that we are victims.

Women are not victims of society or any relationship. We are not helpless.

I don't choose to be a victim.

I don't want to play the victim card.

It might feel sometimes that I have no choice or no control, but I do.

Let me not get tempted to say, "What can I do? I'm a woman.

What can a woman do?"

I will make the choice of standing up and speaking for myself.

I strongly feel we are in the middle of the bridge. In this journey towards having our rights, which are due for many years, we have travelled halfway. So, I often find some women using this perfectly to their benefit.

They take advantage of all the laws meant for their protection and at times use them for their convenience. Also, taking advantage of the orthodox social norms that give them a special status as women. So, either accept that we are equal and quit taking advantage of orthodox norms that give special benefits to us or accept that we don't deserve to get equal treatment.

There are subtle examples in our society, but we won't notice them since we subconsciously think women are truly victims. No, we are not. As I repeat this to myself, the reason is, I vehemently oppose being opportunistic because that is how we lose respect for the word 'feminism'.

Victim card:

Georgina Sturmer shares that when we feel sorry for ourselves, we feel powerless and helpless. We blame others for our situation and current state of affairs.

Things don't end here. We do everything possible and say anything to keep ourselves in the position of a victim. We hurt ourselves by doing so, refuse to take help, and say no one can help us.

"When we think about a victim, we often think about innocent victims. Someone who has experienced something negative or traumatic through no fault of their own.

But victim mentality is something entirely different. It's about how we see ourselves and our default patterns in relationships."

— Georgina Sturmer (Source: 'Victim Mentality': How to identify and cope with it', published in the Medical News Today.)

Imagine when we feel sorry for ourselves and pity ourselves, how much of our self-confidence is harmed? It is the worst way to hurt ourselves; rather, we get so used to this approach that it starts feeling convenient to be in that position. We also get so fatalistic at times. I remember my friend pouring her heart out to me and saying,

"A woman's life is all about sacrificing happiness. It is all about our karma. The other day, my friend booked a movie ticket for me. But, my mother-in-law asked me to instead cancel the plan to attend someone's funeral. You know what I mean, Lin. It's always like that."

But let's just accept it, we need to put our foot down and say, "I will make my choices and never look at myself like a victim. It is my life. I will choose how to live it!"

Many women, when they marry, find the food cooked in the house not suitable to their taste. So, they starve. Or they just get used to eating what is already cooked in the new home, which they absolutely detest. Well, absolutely not needed. You can simply cook food of your choice and eat whatever you wish. You need not force yourself to compromise or give up all your old eating habits. Often, when you marry and start living with your husband, the new family fails to appreciate you. In the desire to get acknowledgement, you start doing more housework - work really hard to impress them. This is how you play the game of a victim.

Let's accept that we unknowingly play the victim card at times.

One of my male friends shared with me,

"If you don't happen to know something about facilitation, just use your charm."

I got furious and fired him, "Dare if you say anything like that. I will break your face. Won't hesitate a bit to thrash you."

He curtly replied, "Linnet, you have reached a stage where you cannot take feedback from people."

I remained stern, "You have reached a point where you cannot give feedback."

This was it. I refused to be a victim and quietly listen to his accusations and sexist remarks. I revolted and put my point through.

Malala chose not to be bogged down by terrorist groups.

She was speaking strongly and openly for the education rights of girls in Pakistan, and this made her a target. When she was returning home after school, a masked gunman shot her. She was admitted to the hospital in Birmingham, UK. When she recovered, she had a choice:

Either live a quiet life or begin the new life she was given. She was determined to fight until every girl could go to school. She then established a charity organisation called Malala Fund to give girls an opportunity to achieve the future they choose.

It is certainly all about making a choice.

"My first exposure to sanitation issues occurred when I got admission to an Engineering college. They probably didn't want to admit me and informed me that there was no ladies toilet in the college. I was adamant and pursued my studies in Engineering at that very college."

– Sudha Murthy.

Had Sudha Murthy cribbed and complained about living in an unequal and male-dominated society, she would never have become an Engineer. But she chose to stick to her guns and realise her dreams.

So, women do have a choice!

A part of the lovely song, 'Wonder Woman' by Lion Babe, says it all.

Songwriters: Pharrell Williams, Lucas Goodman, Jillian Hervey

Wonder Woman lyrics © More Water From Nazareth, EMI Pop Music Publishing, Lion Babe LLC.

"I'm feeling funny, feeling high

They looking at me, I don't mind

Now it is easy to walk on by

I don't want what you got, so you better move along

I ain't gonna break for that

I'm a Wonder Woman (watch out!)

I ain't gonna take all that

I'm a Wonder Woman (watch out)

That'll get you nowhere

You don't wanna see what happens when I get provoked

You don't wanna go there

See me spin around, see me swing my golden rope

Oh, I got power (Wonder Woman powers)

I see signs

They shouting "Honey, (Wonder Woman powers) Watch your behind!"

They can't catch me (watch out, watch out)

Cause I'm too strong

They all want what I got

Never leaving me alone

I ain't gonna break for that

I'm a Wonder Woman (watch out!)

I ain't gonna take all that

I'm a Wonder Woman (watch out)

You don't wanna go there

Trying to confuse me,

say I need you when I know I don't

That'll get you nowhere

Go on and try me,

you can't catch me,

you are just blowing smoke.

So no matter the opposition, the hurdles, if you choose to stand up and fight, you will win or overcome the feeling that you are a victim.

Lately, there have even been cases of generalisation that men always assault a woman, or the woman is always the victim being on the receiving end. Not necessarily, a man can be a victim, too.

When women play the victim card, they don't take responsibility for their own life. They want to be cajoled, and they seek sympathy. In reality, they are playing it so smartly by choosing not to choose.

> **"If it is never our fault, we can't take responsibility for it. If we can't take responsibility for it, we'll always be its victim."**
>
> **– Richard Bach**

May it be divorce cases, marital rape, or infidelity, a woman has the chance to walk out of the marriage, especially if she is financially stable. Then why do women stick to these relationships and act as victims? Why do they choose to be in a relationship that is clearly not meant for them? Now, women have been increasingly aware of their rights and have been speaking up, but we do see women not moving out of these relationships to take control of the situation at times.

In a patriarchal society where women are dependent on men and seen as inferior, most of the time, they are likely to be on the receiving end and experience assaults, rapes, sexual harassment, and discrimination. But does this victim mentality help us to get empowered or make us meek?

Also, we use sarcasm as a weapon and a means to express ourselves. Are we powerless to not express our thoughts clearly and distinctly? We are not powerless. The resentment we face from everyone discourages us from speaking up.

There are many women who have overcome obstacles and moved ahead to see success, because they chose not to feel like a victim, but rather feel empowered by fighting, making a way for themselves and innumerable other women.

The word 'victim' makes you vulnerable and powerless. But are we women so helpless? This view makes a woman passive and demeans her capacity to revolt, fight back, and thrive in adverse situations.

Are we fragile? Are we weak? Are we deficient?

When we adorn the garb of a victim, we say 'yes' to all these questions, but it takes away the will to fight, makes us dependent on someone else, and we always look out for support. We begin to feel powerless, and others too look at us in that manner.

If we shed this garb, we surely start looking at ourselves in a different manner, and the world too changes its view towards us.

At a deeper level, I wish to ask, "Do we women like to be called victims?"

"Do we wish to be called helpless?"

If we fight for empowerment, then the word 'victim' should not be used!

Of course, in cases like rape, sexual abuse, and marital rape, women are victims but not forever. We have the power to heal, and the perpetrators need to be punished. But we have a choice not to live with abuse; we have a choice to walk out and speak for ourselves.

This is what Mary Kom had to say about her adversities.

***"Looking back now, I realise that belonging to
the family of a labourer actually helped to prepare
my body for boxing. There were many times when
my family didn't have enough food or warm clothing
to go around. All this made me physically, as well as
emotionally, tough."***

- Mary Kom

Nothing came easy for Mary Kom. She had to help her parents in the fields, take care of her siblings, go to school, and look after her house.

She says,

> **"I would still say that responsibilities were few at that early age."**
>
> **"Then came boxing, and yes, it wasn't easy for me to keep moving ahead as most people saw it as a male sport, including my parents. Moreover, my diminutive size made it more difficult for me to convince all that boxing was what I was made for. It took a lot to get past those initial hurdles and get involved with the sport wholeheartedly."**

Task

Let's all ask ourselves in any situation, do you say, "I can't do this because I don't have support?"

Let me share with you an incident.

I'm a consultant, so my calendar is all well-planned. My sister, who would take care of my son, was busy, and I was so worried about my son since work travel is lined up throughout the year. I was worried. Who would take care of him?

It was my friend who pointed out to me that I'm a professional and I should have had a list of crèches if such a situation would arise. He said that I was unprepared. I began giving excuses and portrayed myself as a victim. But he was right – I had a solution and needed to be well-prepared for such a challenge.

Are there instances when you have done something like that? Think about it and write down your experience as well.

Positive self-talk.

I'm the creator of my life.

I have the power to make my decisions.

Today, I made a choice to change the narrative of being a victim.

I'm not a victim.

In fact, I possess the power, intellect, and spirit to make choices and fulfil my dreams.

Chapter 7

Gender-Neutral

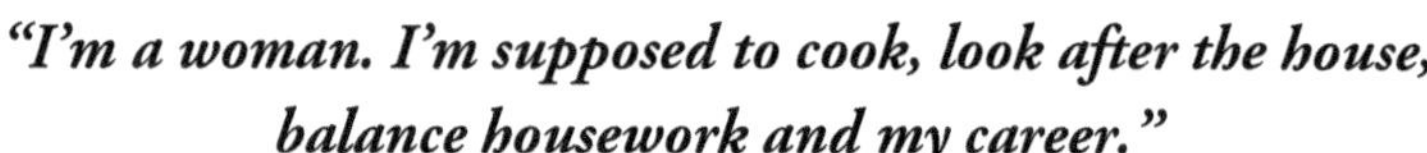

"I'm a woman. I'm supposed to cook, look after the house, balance housework and my career."

"The world is a sadly dangerous place for women and girls,"

"I have so much to do. Oh, I'm so exhausted," said Sasha.

"Why are you doing it alone? Is there no one at home to help you?" asked Vicky.

"Everyone is resting," shouted Sasha.

"And I think young women are tired of it.
They're tired of being undervalued.
They're tired of being disregarded."
- Michelle Obama

We might think Michelle Obama has achieved so much because she is Barack Obama's wife. Let's remind ourselves that she is a law graduate from Harvard Law School; she has worked as a Community Outreach Coordinator at the University of Chicago. Later, she joined as the Staff of the Chicago Office of the Mayor and worked on Community Development and Public Initiatives before she married Barack Obama. She had achieved a lot even before she married. As an individual, she was and is powerful, not because she is Barack Obama's wife, but because she carries that potential and passion.

Women often have to face comments that undervalue their ability and potential, giving credit to men in their lives. Yes, support from people around us is appreciated, but that doesn't imply that a woman doesn't possess the potential to achieve her dreams.

Often at home, we hear things like:

"Get water for your husband or brother. He just returned home tired."

"You are a girl, so cooking is something that you should know."

"Oh, you don't know how to cook. You are a woman." "Don't serve burnt chapati to Dad. I will eat it."

"Let the men finish eating after the Pooja; we women can have lunch later."

"We cannot pay for your trip. Your brother's tuition fees have to be paid."

"We cannot pay your fees anymore. Anyhow, you will marry and leave this house. You are *Paraya Dhan* (belonging to someone else)."

"If you had a brother, things would have been easier for your family."

"Don't back answer; you are a girl."

"I was very fortunate to be raised in a family where there was no difference between my brother and me. We were both given equal opportunities. After parents, it goes into schools, where girls [should be] given a safe environment to dream big, to think big, to value themselves. That is how empowerment will happen."

– Priyanka Chopra

So, let's teach our children that rights are equal to all.

In the process of achieving her dreams, a woman often has to face innumerable impediments. For example, getting an education for many girls is tough as their brothers are given first preference to get educated. Girls are supposed to do housework, and boys are meant to go to school, work, and earn money. We might deny this reality, but in rural India, the divide is clear and right in the face.

Girls in urban India face unique challenges. My friend wished to go abroad to pursue higher education. Her parents set a condition: "If you wish to go abroad to study, marry, and then you are free to go wherever you wish to."

After getting married, she was forced to study at the same University where her partner was studying, despite the fact that she had an opportunity to study at a better University. The reason being she should be with her husband. Furthermore, when she delivered a baby, she had to depend on her parents to raise the child since her in-laws refused to take the child's responsibility.

It is clear: a woman is alone in her journey towards being independent and successful. However, she can put her foot down and make her choices. All she needs to do is voice her opinions, thoughts, and wishes.

Let's study why girls quit school education.

The patriarchal system is embedded in our society so seamlessly, more so in the rural part of India. The article, 'Girls dropout of school due to early marriage, housework', published in the Times of India, mentions:

The National Family Health Survey – 5 (2019-21), reveals that early marriages and chores at home are the main reasons for girls to drop out of school. Out of over 21,800 girls dropped out of school before the year 2019-20, over 13% did so because their help was required for housework.

Almost 7% dropped out of school as they were getting married despite the fact that child marriage is illegal.

It is apparent that gender divide, patriarchy, and economic factors are the main reasons for children to drop out of school. The percentage of girls who dropped out of school to help with housework was over 13%; for boys, it was close to 10%.

The main cause for school dropout of 7% of girls was underage marriage, and for boys, it was 0.3%.

1.7% chose not to go to school due to improper school facilities for girls, and 2% due to safety concerns.

Imagine the impact of not being educated on the life of the girl. She is bereft of all the opportunities she could have got if she educated herself. But the reasons that stop her are apparent from the study above. She sacrifices her education for the family and also because a male member in the family is the priority.

The right to education is basic for everyone and is gender-neutral. So why do girls have to drop out of school?

But we have inspirational women in our country who fought for this cause and were liberated in the true sense.

Dr. Muthulakshmi Reddy:

She passed her matriculation exams with high scores and wished to continue her education by getting admission to college. She applied to the college in Pudukkottai, but she was denied admission due to societal pressure. In those days, women were not allowed to pursue higher education.

Martanda Bhairav Thondaman, the Raja of Pudukkottai, supported her dream and asked the college authorities to grant admission. Thus, Dr. Reddy became the first Indian woman to graduate in Medicine.

Also, she boldly fought against the Devadasi system in our country. The law, called The Madras Devadasi Act, was based on the bill proposed by Dr. Muthulakshmi Reddy in 1930.

She is also the first woman to become a member of the legislature in India. She recommended the Government of India to raise the marriageable age for women. The 'Avvai Home' was her rebellion to shelter women and children who were not protected by society. She housed women who were rescued from the brothel. She ensured the passing of a bill that could remove brothels and stop women and children trafficking. Dr. Reddy also opened a hostel for Muslim girls and pioneered a scholarship for Harijan girls.

Savitribai Phule:

Savitribai Phule is a game-changer in the feminist movement in India and contributed immensely to the cause of education. She was the first female teacher in India (way back in 1848) and established a school for girls along with her husband, Jyotiba Phule, during a time when women's education was strongly opposed in Indian society. She also opened a shelter for destitute women in 1864. The Phules opened an education society that started many more schools for women.

Along with Jyotiba Phule, she established the Satyashodhak Samaj, which aimed at removing discrimination from society. In 1873, they both started conducting marriages called the Satyashodhak Marriage. In this unique concept, the couples took an oath of equality and education. This was how both Savitribai Phule and Jyotiba Phule played a revolutionary role in India. Savitribai defied all social norms, and lit Jyotiba's funeral pyre at a time when women didn't have the right to do so. She continued the legacy and took over Satyashodhak Samaj. We can never forget the significant contribution of Savitribai Phule and Jyotiba Phule, as they fought for the cause of women and faced severe opposition but didn't give up.

Also, a few anecdotes that have stayed with me in the past few years have made me ponder about gender neutrality.

I still remember having been invited to a friend's house, where they were hosting the *Kajal* ceremony. It is a ceremony where the child is applied kajal to protect against the evil eye. The ceremony was being held, and the child's grandmother casually said, "My neighbour was invited to apply kajal. I mean, she is a daughter, after all. If I had a grandson, I would have called my sister from Kolkata and hosted a big ceremony." She didn't feel she was discriminating; in fact, she was pretty casual about it.

I've heard people discriminate without feeling they are doing so. For example, in our neighbourhood, a family has two children - a boy and a girl. Their grandparent once said something subtly discriminating, "If my grandson asks for palak paneer late at night, we cook it for him. But our granddaughter is a very understanding child; she eats anything."

Thus, it is clearly evident that the grandson's wishes are more important to her.

So, now let's look at another gender-neutral value – that is the right to nutrition.

This is a study done by UNICEF.

"Women have the right to food and nutrition throughout their lives – a right that is enshrined in multiple international Human Rights instruments. A woman's nutritional status is a powerful barometer of her well-being. A well-nourished woman has a strong immune system and nutrient reserves to buffer the effects of infection, while meeting her additional nutrient needs during pregnancy or breastfeeding."

"A well-nourished woman is more likely to have well-nourished infants and young children who join her on a path to good health and prosperity. However, this is not the reality that many women experience, as triple threats of undernutrition (underweight and short stature), micronutrient deficiencies, and overweight affect women across the world."

Sharmistha Chakraborty says in her article "**India Suffers Because Women Eat The Last And The Least**," published in Planet Outlook in 2019:

"With every second woman anaemic, every third woman with a low Body Mass Index (BMI), and every fourth child born with low birth weight, the malnutrition situation in India is staggering."

The quality of lives is primarily dependent on women's health and nutrition. It determines the survival of the future generations of a country. A healthy diet is a must, and so is access to health services to address the micronutrient deficiencies leading to poor health and diseases.

Sharmistha questions, "Is it only nutrition?" Researchers are trying to investigate social indices that impact a woman's nutrition and health. Women navigate through the patriarchal system despite the fact that we claim to be progressive.

Girls are eligible to become a wife and mother. Their education then becomes restricted, and the opportunities do too. Studies show that there is a strong relationship between access to education and a reduction in undernutrition.

Early marriage and teenage pregnancy are threats, especially for rural women. Forty-seven percent of girls marry at the age of 18 years, and most of them soon become mothers at a tender age, as per the 2007 report released by the Indian Institute of Population Studies.

So, adolescent women getting pregnant, who are already undernourished have dire consequences on the overall health, nutritional status, and mental health of young girls.

Infant mortality:

"India's female Infant Mortality Rate (IMR), drops to the same level as males," an article published in The Times of India penned by Rema Nagarajan mentions:

India is the only country in the world where more girls below the age of one die than boys. But in 2020, the female Infant Mortality Rate (IMR) equalised with male IMR. However, in 16 states, IMR has been higher for female babies than males. But now the gap seems to have reduced.

What is the Infant Mortality Rate?

It is the number of infant deaths for every 1,000 live births.

The scenario in rural India is not encouraging, though. The female IMR remains very high compared to that of the male IMR.

Also, women generally neglect their health, and it becomes a challenge for them after they hit menopause. They are more prone to ovarian cancer as the progesterone levels fall.

Menopause also affects the bone marrow. Diet plays an important role, and women tend to neglect it all through their lives, taking more care of their families.

All said and done, once they begin to earn, do they have the liberty to invest and spend money? We know that women, after marriage, drop out of the workforce, especially after they become mothers.

"It's a mystery: Women in India drop out of the workforce even as the economy grows," an article penned by Lauren Frayer and Raksha Kumar on NPR mentions:

The World Bank revealed in its 2021 study that fewer than 1 in 5 Indian women work - at least formally. In India, most work is informal in the form of agriculture and domestic work, which doesn't get counted.

In India, the female labour participation rate shows a steady downward curve from 32% in 2005 to 19% in 2021. While India is developing, the dropout from the workforce is high, be it rich or poor women, urban or rural women across social or religious classes, and age groups.

But there have been women who have made a place for themselves by holding powerful positions that are usually held by men.

Let us continue with our examples of women who have broken the barriers of gender discrimination. Another strong example is Margaret Thatcher.

Margaret Thatcher:

Known for her economic policies named Thatcherism, she was called the 'Iron Lady' due to her uncompromising nature and leadership style. As the Prime Minister of the United Kingdom from 1979 to 1990, she was the longest-serving British Minister of the 20th century. Along with this achievement, she was also the first woman to become the Prime Minister of the United Kingdom.

The economic policies that she implemented intended to reverse the high inflation rate in the country and the recession too. Her economic policies were focused on individual liberty, privatisation of companies that were owned by the State. Her policies aimed at reducing the influence of trade unions in the state and their impact on the economy. Her task was tough, and she took tough steps to stabilise the economy of the country.

Indira Gandhi:

The only female Prime Minister of India, Indira Gandhi, took some courageous decisions for the country. Her leadership led to a Military conflict that resulted in repelling Chinese incursions in the Himalayas in 1967. She declared war against Pakistan in 1971, which was instrumental in the formation of Bangladesh. Indira Gandhi was known to be a powerful woman all around the world, and was known as 'Mother Indira' due to her support of the Green Revolution, the call to combat poverty, and propelling the economy in the early 1980s.

She was named the 'Woman of the Millennium' by BBC in an online poll. Later in 2020, she was among the 100 women responsible for defining the past century by the Times Magazine.

Sania Mirza:

We all know Sania Mirza's achievement as a tennis player and the pride of Indian tennis. This is what she had to say at a panel discussion organised as part of the 35th annual session of the FICCI Ladies Organisation, called 'Women Shaping the Future.'

"As much as we talk about women's empowerment and equality (with men), I feel we still live in a man's world to a large extent,"

"I have been saying for a long time that women should be paid equal prize money to men. This discrimination is present in all sports worldwide. My question is, why do we even need to explain that women should have equal prize money to men? I want to reach the day when we don't need to explain this."

The question is about how many women can have promising careers due to the innumerable challenges they face in their lives.

In an article, 'It's a mystery: Women in India drop out of the workforce even as the economy grows,' published in the NPR in 2023 it is mentioned:

Sher Verick, an economist from the International Labour Organisation, conducted a seminal 2014 study. Female labour in India has continued to decline.

Economists mention six factors that explain this phenomenon:

- Prosperity
- Education
- Social norms
- Safety concerns
- Problems with statistical measurement
- Lack of decent and productive employment

Let us discuss a few of these points

A.L. Sharada, a Sociologist, Demographer, and Director of Population First - a social welfare group based in Mumbai, says that women leave the workforce when the economy grows, as they work only as standby or in case of an emergency. It is not because they wilfully want to have a career. So, when financially, a family does well, they quit or retreat. Yes, we seem to be progressive, yet a lot of Indians are conservative when it comes to the role of women in the family.

She mentions that family becomes the first priority for many women across the world but more so in India. The glorified image of women as mothers sacrificing, caring, and nurturing impacts their role. The other aspects of their personality like a competitor or achiever with aspirations are not given much importance.

When statistics show India's female labour rate is around 20%, it doesn't imply that 80% of women aren't working. Women do a lot of unpaid work like looking after the household, planting and harvesting on farms - these are works that aren't counted.

Verick states that the primary issue is the lack of ability of the economy to create decent, productive employment appropriate and accessible for women.

Some things are absolutely gender-neutral, like teaching boys to cook, clean, respect elders, respect women, help elders, values, financial knowledge, good health, etc. In these matters, no compromises and discrimination should be made especially while raising your children.

Children need not begin feeling that some tasks are not needed to be done by men or women need not do certain tasks. Only when these values are imbibed among children, will society change. I strongly believe mothers play the role of a catalyst in creating a gender-neutral society.

Tasks

List the things that you feel women cannot accomplish and men can.

Think rationally if you are gender-neutral when it comes to these activities.

Share your thoughts with some of your female friends, male friends, and family - if you have a partner and children.

Attempt to consciously do away with gender-discriminating thoughts.

Positive Talk: A Promise

The desire to become gender-neutral will include me asking many uncomfortable questions.

I will begin asking these questions to myself and begin to voice my opinion.

I will venture outside my comfort zone. And speak in favour of gender neutrality.

Chapter 8

Fight for Your Rights

"Asking for what I deserve is being too demanding."

Sasha said, "Women don't have rights. They only have duties."

"Oh, let's see!" challenged Vicky.

Sasha fell while playing and got up again. This repeated a couple of times.

But she didn't give up, and Vicky was surprised.

"I thought girls are weak and give up!"

And all the boys laughed.

"We (women) broke societal norms only to tie us down by indulging in self-doubt, self-pity, and self-restraint. We spread our wings, but did not take the flight."

– Pratibha (Pat), Founder of Refract Consulting

On a quiet evening, as I sat together over some drinks with a dear friend of mine, we got into a heated debate. She said,

"Women don't have it in them to reach the top. Otherwise, we would have more women there."

I got a bit upset and retorted, "Women don't get enough opportunities or support, so I think you are wrong."

"Oh, come on, how long are you going to behave like a crybaby and complain?" she blurted out.

I simply called off the evening. "Let's meet after a month and find out in the meantime, the truth about why women aren't there at the top positions?"

"See ya!!"

We parted ways, and my studies began.

I found from a lot of reading and talking to people, that women earn less on average than men in the same position, and they are underrepresented in the top positions. Women also get less than they deserve as they don't ask for more. They stay satisfied with less.

Women feel apprehensive asking for what they wish or need.

They don't fight for their personal space. If they need their space and want to be alone while they work from home, they will never ask for it. Even if they need to be alone for a while, they will not ask for it - like men are entitled to sit in peace either for work or otherwise - women, too, need to have that personal space. Women should fight for their personal space.

One of my close friends was brought up lovingly by her parents. Her elder sister got married to a rich, highly educated, and wealthy family. After marriage, she migrated to Singapore. But the family didn't seem liberated. She was asked to serve food to the family first; after they finished, she could have her lunch. Despite being in the highest position in a company, she decided not to voice her opinion and adjust as most women do. She decided not to fight for her rights.

My friend decided not to marry looking at the state of affairs in her sister's life. Ultimately, when she got married, she faced the same type of discrimination. Her in-laws insisted that she come home early from work. Gradually, she faced mental abuse - she broke down completely. The person I knew was a kind soul, always full of energy and vitality. She was no longer that happy and vibrant person. She finally got divorced, but her in-laws had killed her spirit and desire to live. Later, she moved on but had to pay a huge price as she had lost the charm and sparkling personality she had earlier.

In the book 'Women Don't Ask: Negotiation and the Gender Divide', authors Linda Babcock and Lara Laschever study the barriers that hold women back and the social forces that constrain them.

- Their study showed that women don't want to negotiate. Their survey showed that 2.5 times more women than men said they feel apprehensive about negotiating.

- Men initiate negotiations around four times more often than women.

- Women are pessimistic about what is available, so when they begin negotiating, they ask for less and get less too. They negotiate 30% less than men.

- 20% of adult women say they never negotiate, despite the fact that they consider negotiation appropriate and necessary.

- Women most often feel so grateful for being offered a job that they accept what they are offered and never negotiate their salary.

- Not knowing the market value of their work is common among women. They report salary expectations between 3 to 32 percent lower than men for the same jobs. Men expect 13% more earnings than women during the first year of full-time work, and 32% more at the peak of their careers.

My Reflections:

I believe that if you settle for mediocrity, you will never realise your full potential and keep underestimating yourself. It undermines your potential. When you give up on business or a job or accept a job that has no growth potential, you are stuck and feel settled even if you get less.

You accept less, you will always get less.

Now that we know these facts, let's not make the same mistakes again. Let's ask for what we want.

Marriott International held a conference on Women in Leadership. Incidentally, it's the only hotel company to be led by a woman in India. Ranju Alex, the Area Vice-President, South Asia, Marriott International Inc., spoke to ET Hospitality World, and the article is penned by Bikramjit Ray, titled "What we need as women is an equal seat at the table and to be heard."

Here are the snippets of the interview.

- Ranju said that they realised at the starting level there are many women in hospitality. So, in a hotel school, you will have anywhere between 30 to 50 percent of women learning. But at the top, there is nobody. This implies that in their work life, women lose steam. Or they fail to cope with the pressure and leave.

- The problem is not with the women not choosing to work in this industry. It is about giving them a platform and workplace flexibility in a way that it becomes suitable for them to continue working.

- This happens between the ages of around 27 to 35 when women mostly marry and think about starting a family. Women give up during this period. They choose to be at home to look after children.

- Our society is responsible for ensuring that women don't step down, which means family and friends should support her. A good supportive childcare system should be available.

- Companies should provide flexibility in work timings, understand their challenges, and pair up with a buddy who has already gone through these challenges in life to guide the person.

- We have to understand what she is going through to work out things.

- The whole theme is about not using gender as an excuse or a ladder. Women should get facilities or promotions not because they are women. What women want is an equal seat at the table and wish to be heard.

- Merit then takes its course. We want an equal opportunity to present ourselves and to speak our minds.

My Reflections:

Women deserve a seat at the table, not because they are women, but because they face unique challenges and possess the potential to contribute immensely to a company, economy, and society as a whole.

So, their challenges should be understood; the support system should be made available to them, and then they can be promoted based on their merit. Women don't want favours, but just need to be understood and get the necessary support.

If this is possible, women will not settle for less or quit. They will be encouraged to contribute and grow. Though they should learn to ask for what they want. If they don't ask, they will never get what they want.

A research paper titled,

Excerpts from "Do women give up competing more easily? Evidence from the Lab and the Dutch Math Olympiad," authored by Thomas Buser and Huaiping Yuan, published in the American Economic Journal: Applied Economics.

- Women are more likely than men to stop competing if they lose. This is what the lab experiments and field data from the Dutch Math Olympiad reveal.

- In the lab Math competition, women are much less likely than men to choose competition again after they lose in the first round.

- Girls, but not boys, who fail to enter the second round are less likely to participate and compete again after a year.

- This gender difference in the reaction to competition can help to tell us why fewer women make it to the top in business and academia.

Based on this study, an article was published on the website of the London School of Economics and Political Science by the same authors, which reveals:

Why are women underrepresented at the top of both academia and the corporate world?

They represent only 25% of professors in the UK and 5% of Fortune 500 CEOs. They say that data from the Dutch Math Olympiad implies that results hold true outside the lab.

- Economists measure the readiness to compete in the lab by offering people a choice between different rewards for their performance in a task.

- One has to choose between a reward based on one's performance, and receiving a higher reward if a person performs better than the other participant.

- When women are given this choice, they tend to choose the safer, non-competitive option.

- The reaction to losing was even more interesting among top performers. High-performing men rarely get impacted by a loss in the first round, while high-performing women (56%) are less likely to enter the competition again after facing a loss.

- Women are less inclined or interested in competing with others in the first place. Even those who are willing to compete, if they face a setback, don't persevere.

- This shows that high performers initially agreeing to compete are those whom we can expect to have the potential to be at the top of their careers.

- Thus, the experiment shows that high-potential women are likely to be losing out as they quit too early.

It had been a month, and I met my friend again, and this is what I shared with her, which she too agreed to.

Women fight but give up very quickly. Women make compromising negotiations.

Women take lesser offers. We don't fight for equality.

We are told we don't need to earn a lot or become super successful or aim for more, as husbands will take care of us.

When we speak our minds, we are called dominating, demanding, loud, and boisterous.

I also strongly believe that women should be financially independent. They should earn and have the right to invest as per their choice. Financial independence brings confidence and a sense of achievement. Women should not be bereft of this feeling. They need not ask their father or their husband for money or depend on them for financial advice.

I want to say this loud and clear:

You deserve a seat at the table. You deserve equal pay.

You deserve an equal status at work.

You will always get less if you don't ask for it. Settling for less will become a habit.

You didn't start this fight to attempt to try; you fought to win.

Tasks

Write down your dreams and prepare a solid plan to achieve them.

Write down why it is important for you to achieve this dream.

List all the people whose support you need in this journey and share with them what kind of support you expect.

Keep a target for yourself and deadlines as well.

At each juncture when you wish to give up, ask yourself, "Why did you begin this journey?"

Positive Talk

I believe in myself. I'm not weak – I'm strong enough to get there and complete the journey that I embarked on.

I can make my own decisions; some situations will be more demanding in business and at work, but I will take up these challenges to win over them.

I will ask for support whenever needed, assert that I need to win, and achieve my dreams.

Building a support system to help me overcome challenges will be my priority.

Settling for less is not what I wish for. My needs are important to me, and I will not sacrifice my dreams for anyone or anything.

Chapter 9

Multi-Tasking is Not Only for Women; Sacrifice is Not a Virtue

*"You are a woman so multi-tasking
comes naturally to you."*

Sasha was on the swing, and her friend kept waiting for his turn.

Sasha sacrificed for her friend and got down from the swing.

Vicky asked her, "Why did you give up the swing for him?"

Sasha said, "My mum says it's good to sacrifice."

"Oh really, but I never do," said Vicky.

*"The human mind was not designed to multitask.
We're actually switching from one task to another very
rapidly. And every time we do, there's a cognitive cost in
terms of time and mental resources."*

- David Meyer, cognitive psychologist

Brontë sisters:

Emily Brontë wrote under the name of Ellis Bell, Anne Brontë under the name of Acton Bell, and Charlotte Brontë as Currer Bell. The Brontë sisters became famous in the world of English literature but not by their own names. They had to publish their work under male names. This has been mentioned in the preface of Wuthering Heights.

"We did not like to declare ourselves women because - at that time suspecting that our mode of writing and thinking was not what is called 'feminine'—we had a vague impression that Authoresses are liable to be looked on with prejudice."

Conclusively, the sisters were well aware that publishing their novels under male names would elicit an unbiased response and so would be the critique of their work. If they had published under their names, it would be impacted by sexism.

So, women were not accepted to venture into professions that were typically meant for men. They were criticised and never accepted.

Little women:

The novel 'Little Women', written by Louisa May Alcott, portrays the lives of the March sisters - Meg, Jo, Beth, and Amy - living in Massachusetts. Set in the 19th century, when women were not appreciated or encouraged to pursue any art forms, the sisters were confident that they could make a name for themselves. The Editor who agreed to publish her novel said, "If the main character is a girl, make sure she gets married at the end of the novel."

One of the dialogues in the movie says it all. It represents the voice of many challenges that women faced in the 18th century:

"As a woman, there is no way I can make my own money. Not enough to earn a living or disappoint my family. And if I had that money, which I don't, that money would belong to my husband the moment we got married. If we had children, they would be his, not mine. They would be his property. So don't sit there and say marriage is not an economic proposition because it is."

One more example is that of the women in Medinipur. Medinipur is a district in India that made an active contribution to the Indian Independence Movement and fought against British colonialism. The role of women, especially the commercial sex workers in this region, in the Indian freedom struggle is not popularly known to people. It rarely finds mention in any of the history books – their sacrifices go unacknowledged even after so many years of independence.

These prejudices seep deeply into our minds.

Most mothers will teach their daughters to be sacrificial.

These are some prejudiced remarks that we hear at home and around us.

While a woman is at her desk working from home, she is disturbed many a time for some household chore or when children need her. It is never the man who is asked to help. Apparently, he would get disturbed while working.

"Mum, I need something to eat." "Listen na, get me some tea."

"Put the baby to sleep; she is cranky."

"Clean the utensils as I have a meeting,"

This became common and quite evident during the pandemic. Women were doing double duties, taking care of the house and managing office work from home.

We give space to men while they are at their desks and focused on work. But do we give that same liberty to a woman? She is supposed to prioritise her family first, adjust to others' timetables, and justify all her roles.

If we fail at one – we are often criticised. "Such an insensitive mother she is!"

"Women cannot be great leaders."

"Women deserve to be in the kitchen. They can't handle the work stress and challenges of a corporate career."

Is that true?

Let's find that out later in this chapter.

There are anecdotes, conversations, and dialogues that we often hear, and they have become a part of our daily lives.

The conversations are about women being more sacrificial.

Women being more giving, when it comes to making compromises, we are at the forefront. The world has glorified the act of sacrificing among women since it helps to maintain the status quo.

We women are masters at multi-tasking. We are great at juggling between household chores, family, and career. But isn't it obvious that if we do all of this simultaneously, we are bound to fail at one point?

Also, why do we have to multi-task? Does it come naturally to women?

Multi-tasking is perceived to be a part of a woman's domain traditionally. She can juggle between household chores, responsibilities and her career. Organising appointments for children and at work, social arrangements, packing lunch boxes, attending parent meetings, cooking, cleaning, and focusing on her career – all this comes naturally to women.

No, it doesn't. A new study published in PLOS One (journal) shows women are actually no better at multi-tasking than men. The study tested whether women were better at switching between tasks and managing multiple tasks at the same time. But the results were surprising. Women's brains are not more efficient than men at either of these functions/tasks.

So multi-tasking doesn't come naturally to women. In fact, the belief that women are great at multi-tasking, burdens them with myriad responsibilities.

The corporate world exploits women by handing them roles that include multi-tasking under the pretext that women are great at multi-tasking.

But women accept these roles because we compromise and accept what is offered. We don't know how to say no and overstretch our boundaries. Among women, the need for approval is so high that they cannot say 'no'.

Sacrifice is not necessarily a virtue. It's often said that a woman who sacrifices is a noble woman. But, while sacrificing, her wishes get squashed, and anger and frustration build up. Constant sacrificing isn't healthy for your happiness.

"What is good for gender equality is good for the economy and society as well. The COVID-19 pandemic puts that truth into stark relief and raises critically important choices."

- McKinsey Report

The research paper, 'Women's Well-being and the burden of unpaid work', penned by Soraya Seedat and Marta Rondon, studies how gender inequities in time allocated to unpaid work became a cause of concern during the COVID-19 pandemic, thus affecting their mental health.

- Women spend more amount of time carrying out three-quarters of the world's unpaid work.

- The care and domestic work taken up by women globally is three times more than that of men, while women in low- and middle-income countries spend more time in unpaid work compared to high-income countries.

- Globally, unpaid care work is considered low value and is not accounted for in mainstream economics. This is due to the deep-rooted patriarchal institutions and accounting systems that fail to record women's contributions.

- Women do unpaid domestic work, and it has a greater impact on mental health, negatively affecting the quality of life.

- During the pandemic, time spent on domestic work and care hiked for both men and women – though undeniably, the intensity of this work has been far greater for women.

- The workload has been stressful, so it is going to create an impact on women's mental health.

- The 'double burden' of engaging in a paid job and an unpaid one has different effects. Household work stress affects women more than men. The fact that women do more household chores, became apparent during the COVID-19 pandemic. Asymmetry in gender during the pandemic that extended to childcare, with mothers engaging in more childcare than fathers, became a worrisome factor.

- Taking care of children became an issue due to the closure of schools and daycare centres and unavailability of home help. Social norms look at women as caregivers and providers. Though unpaid work is clearly associated with poor mental health for women.

In an article titled 'Sacrificing Work for Family: How Do Women and Men Perceive This Sacrifice?' published on the website of the Centre for Mind, Brain, and Behaviour Research (CIMCYC), mentions a study at the Mind, Brain, and Behaviour Research Centre of the University of Granada (UGR). This study was conducted by two researchers from the Social Psychology and Gender Laboratory and the Psychology of Social Problems group.

It is an investigation that analyses the perception of costs and benefits of sacrificing work for family among heterosexual couples.

- Labour participation among women has increased in recent years, but this has not led to a balance of family responsibilities between women and men.

- In recent years, there has been an increase in women's labour participation, but this has not automatically led to a balance in the family responsibilities of women and men.

- Men have not proportionally increased their commitment to the private sphere. Women have reduced their commitment to the public sphere by sacrificing their career aspirations to look after the family.

How is our society perceiving these sacrifices? Why do some women make these decisions of sacrifice?

- We can understand this by analysing the perceived costs and benefits of sacrificing work for the family. Women themselves perceive this decision as beneficial, or their partners perceive it as beneficial. Research revealed that women and men both perceive sacrificing work for the family as more costly for men and beneficial for women.

- Male and female participants perceived that women find it truer to themselves as they make these sacrifices. Women indicated that they are more willing to sacrifice work for family than men.

- This shows that our society has accepted the presence of women in the public sphere. It is socially acceptable for them to sacrifice their presence in the public sphere to protect their private sphere.

- Today's society perpetuates gender inequality in the private sphere. We have yet to achieve equality in this matter.

- Let's look at an example – a personal experience of Grace Jennings-Edquist shared in an article, "In a society that fetishises female self-sacrifice, saying 'no' saved me" in the Guardian.

Let me quote her,

"As a working mother, one word has saved me as the pandemic has worn on: 'No'. I've learned to say no to being the parent who will automatically take carer's leave when childcare centres and schools close. No to being the only one to plan meals for the week. No to being the type of Instagram-worthy mother who mindfully makes her own hummus throughout lockdown."

Saying no has positively impacted her life and fostered a healthy relationship with her partner.

To say 'no', such a short word, is not easy for women because they wish to please people. We have been taught to be accommodating, compromising, and sacrificing. We never say 'no' when we really wish to say it.

> ***"For that reason, feminism has a particular duty to fight 'the tyranny of niceness' – which is, and has always been, one of the most potent forces holding women back. Feminism is not a self-help movement dedicated to making everyone feel better about their lives. It is a radical demand to overturn the status quo."***
>
> ***-Helen Lewis***

We want to be nice and then we refrain from saying no, though we wish to say so. We don't wish to be called rude, selfish, individualistic, and career-obsessed, so we keep saying yes to unrealistic expectations of our family. Let's accept it; we cannot parent children alone, we cannot do all the household chores alone. The work is meant to be shared, and that attitude has to be nurtured among women. Marriage is a partnership; that is what is agreed upon, but we conveniently forget it. But we feel the pressure to hide the fact that we are drained out, frustrated, and angry.

We keep a smiling face, and from within, we have sacrificed more than is needed for our well-being.

What are we sacrificing?

Our self-esteem and well-being.

This kind of system is not sustainable in the long run. It will collapse – either the marriage or the woman. The scenario is gradually changing.

Reversal of gender roles:

Today, gender roles are reversing. Mothers are teaching their sons to cook and also do household chores. Irrespective of gender, every individual has to be independent.

So, to summarise, sacrifice is not a virtue. If sacrifice is affecting our well-being, then it definitely is not a virtue. We begin regretting our sacrifices and repent on the opportunities not taken. The victim mindset that we discuss in this book is closely connected to this sacrificing nature and our lack of self-compassion.

Task:

Honest answers will help you realise your approach - for women.

- Are you doing all the work and getting totally drained out?

  Yes

  No

- How often do you say yes when you really wish to say no?

  Never

  Sometimes

  Quite often

  Always

For both men and women –

- Do you think women should be more sacrificing?

  Yes

  No

- Would you like it if your family member sacrifices her career for handling house responsibilities?

  Yes

  No

- Do you think women are good at multi-tasking?

  Yes

  No

- Do you think it's important for men to know cooking and do household chores?

  Yes

  No

Positive self-talk

Multi-tasking comes naturally to women – this isn't true.

I will not trouble myself by doing multiple tasks and draining out myself.

I will take care of myself – nurture myself and take out time to relax.

Where it is necessary for my well-being, saying 'no' will be my choice.

Saying 'no' might be tough now, but in the long run, it will benefit everyone.

I love myself, so I will not compromise on my mental, emotional, and physical well-being.

Chapter 10

You Have a Right to Nutrition (An Equal Plate is Your Right)

"Look at her plate. She is eating so much.

She is already so fat and gulping so much food."

Sasha's plate was full at the party.

She was busy enjoying her plate full of delicious food.

Vicky's mother looked at her and mumbled,

"Look at the way she is hogging. She doesn't even feel shy to fill her plate with so much food."

Vicky looked confused. "Mum, my plate is full too, but you said nothing to me?"

"Come on, you are a boy; girls don't eat so much. They should not get fat."

"Why, Mum?" queried Vicky.

> ### *"The right to food is not a luxury,*
> ### *it's a fundamental human right."*
>
> ### *- Jean Ziegler*

At our college reunion, one of my female friends was gorging on food, and her plate was full. She was totally enjoying her food when someone made a sly remark,

"Look at her – the way she is eating. Her plate is totally full, and she is eating like a pig."

That came as a shock to me. I immediately hit back, "Well, it's her right to eat as much as she likes. Who are you to judge?"

Bang came the reply, "Generally, girls don't eat so much.

Putting on weight looks ugly as well."

This is a common remark when a woman loves to eat. Women are supposed to eat less, and men more.

Where is this all rooted, and how is it that we subconsciously believe that women eat less?

Thin is a dysmorphic way of saying a person is healthy. Women are judged if they eat more, but don't they have the right to feel full or eat enough as much as their appetite? Women need to speak up and say,

"This is how much I need to eat, and I see nothing wrong in it."

In fact, women need more nutrition after giving birth to a child and during pregnancy too.

Women are iron deficient—

#Fact one:

The ICMR Bulletin published in the year 2000, titled 'Iron Absorption and Its Implications On Strategies to Control Iron Deficiency Anaemia', reveals that,

Iron Deficiency Anaemia is common worldwide, especially in India and other developing countries. Women are most vulnerable to Iron Deficiency Anaemia.

Let's look at the survey results:

- 87% of pregnant women suffer from anaemia.

- About 10% have severe anaemia.

- 16% of maternal deaths are due to anaemia.

- Maternal anaemia is a contributing factor to the following health challenges:
  - Perinatal mortality.
  - Low Birth Weight
  - Foetal Wastage.
  - It also leads to irreversible impairment in the child's learning ability.
  - Other behavioural abnormalities.

#Fact two:

Maternal mortality is extremely high and, in fact, unacceptable.

About 287,000 women lost their lives during and after pregnancy and childbirth in the year 2020. Almost 95% of all maternal deaths happened in low and lower-middle-income countries in 2020. What is even more alarming is that they could have been prevented.

One of the factors that prevent women from getting or seeking care during their pregnancy is:

Harmful gender norms and inequalities lead to giving less importance to the rights of women and girls, including their right to safe, quality, and affordable sexual and reproductive health services.

World Health Organisation mentions that:

- Each day in 2020, almost 800 women lost their lives from preventable causes related to pregnancy and childbirth.

- Almost 95% of maternal deaths happened in low- and lower-middle-income countries in 2020.

- Almost every two minutes, a maternal death occurred in 2020.

- A positive sign: From 2000 to 2020, the Maternal Mortality Ratio (MMR), which means the number of maternal deaths per 100,000 live births, dropped by about 34% worldwide.

- When cared for by skilled health professionals before, during, and after pregnancy, it can save women's lives and the newborns too.

Observer Research Foundation (ORF) mentions:

'Hunger has a woman's face' is a true adage because in two-thirds of all countries, women face more food insecurity compared to men.

- Maternal nutrition is an important factor in supporting pregnancy and impacting maternal, neonatal, and child health outcomes.

- Maternal undernutrition accounts for 20% of stunting among children.

- Poor nutrient intake and poor education, along with low socio-economic status of women, adversely impact behavioural practices with regard to self-care, affecting Body Mass Index (BMI) of pregnant women and foetal growth. It also contributes to undernutrition, i.e., stunting in children.

- The impact of maternal nutrition on child nutrition is acknowledged and is included in programmes for preventing child undernutrition, especially during the first 1000 days of life.

- Poor nutrition among women in adolescence and the pre- conception stage leads to women entering pregnancy undernourished. This leads to serious consequences like impaired foetal development, resulting in babies with low birth weight or being small for gestational age.

- Women who were stunted in childhood remain stunted as adults and have all chances to have stunted children.

NFHS - National Family Health Survey

Women often eat less and are neglected, mostly eating at the end after the family finishes eating their meal. Gender norms lead to unequal distribution and consumption of food by women.

So coming back to the adage 'Hunger has a woman's face', it's observed that in nearly two-thirds of all countries, women face more food insecurity than men. In fact, it is found that India is the only large country in the world where more girl babies die than boy babies. The gender differential in child survival is currently 11 percent.

Some shocking revelations have been made in the article, 'Over Two Lakh Young Girls Die Every Year in India Because of Their Gender', published in The Wire, which are as follows:

- Women are often judged when they eat more. In India, there is a preference for sons that is preventing girls from being born, causing higher mortality among girls who are born.

- A study published in Lancet Global Health reveals:

- On average, about 239,000 girls under the age of five years lose their lives every year in India due to their gender – due to unwanted childbearing and neglect.

- Female foetuses are aborted, and this results in fewer girls being born in our country.

- Premature death of girls is due to neglect, and this figure adds up to an estimated 63 million women missing from the population.

So, we have the right to food?

We should ignore comments like:

"You are eating so much – your plate is full. Are you sure you will be able to finish so much?"

"You will put on weight; check your diet." "Girls don't eat so much. They should eat less." "Men need more food, and women need less."

As children grow up, parents focus on the boy child – they give all the facilities to the boy child first as compared to the girl child. In fact, women eat last in most homes; if there is any religious ceremony being performed, men eat first and women eat after them.

Men get served first, and women are supposed to eat less.

This is an excerpt from the chapter 'Development, Ecology and Women' by Vandana Shiva - physicist, ecologist, fierce advocate of biodiversity and conservation, protector of farmers and women's rights, and prolific author. It indicates how colonialism made things worse for women.

"Ester Boserup has documented how women's impoverishment increased during the colonial rule; those rulers who had spent a few centuries in subjugating and crippling their own women into de-skilled, de-intellectualised appendages, disfavoured the women of the colonies on matters of access to land, technology, and employment. The economic and political processes of colonial underdevelopment bore the clear mark of modern Western patriarchy, and while large numbers of women and men were impoverished by these processes, women tended to lose more."

The privatisation of land for revenue generation displaced women more critically, eroding their traditional land-use rights.

The expansion of cash crops undermined food production, and women were often left with meagre resources to feed and care for children, the aged, and the infirm when men migrated or were conscripted into forced labour by the colonisers.

As a child, my father and brother got a major share of food cooked at home, so I always starved as a child. After I began working, the first thing I did was to eat enough – at parties when I took the second helping, everyone laughed at me. When a woman has a large appetite, she is laughed at. But if that is what she needs, I don't think there should be an objection from anyone. It is rooted deep in our subconscious mind that girls eat less.

In fact, women take care of everyone in the family, but they neglect their own health. In most families, if a woman chooses to eat first, she is labelled selfish. She is questioned if she has served everyone. But I say, "No one has served me – the day anyone shows the courtesy to serve me, I will reciprocate and serve them."

Here, mothers play a major role in bringing up their children to be gender-neutral. Everyone has the right to eat nutritious food – so the male child should not be given preference. Mothers ought to tell their children that the right to food is equal for everyone. If we wish to have our right to food and nutrition, we, as mothers, should teach our kids about gender neutrality. No one gets preferential treatment.

Task:

1. Every time you feel hungry, you should not feel guilty about eating first.

2. Whenever you witness anyone making clichéd remarks about women eating more or some woman having a healthy appetite, do object.

3. Wherever you witness or face gender discrimination, do speak up.

4. Write down your experience of speaking up and the reactions from people around you.

   • Were you called a feminist?

   • Were you called dominating and aggressive?

- Did anyone support you?

5. Also, do write down your idea of feminism: your unique way of describing feminism.

Positive self-talk

I will take care of my health and eat nutritious food.

If I'm hungry, I will eat without sacrificing the food for someone else.

You Have a Right to Nutrition (An Equal Plate is Your Right)

I have a right to food and nutrition – if I don't get my right, I will fight for it.

Not hesitating while I eat – I will ensure I eat enough and don't starve.

My children will be taught the importance of gender neutrality through my own actions.

Chapter 11

Expressing Your Sexuality is a Sin

"I have to conceal my sexuality. To reveal is a sin."

Sasha wore a pretty short dress.

Looking happy, she trotted to Vicky and jumped in excitement.

"Hey, how is my dress?"

Vicky delightedly answered, "It's pretty, just like you!"

"Well, I think it's too short. Why are you showing off your legs?" said his mother.

Note: It all starts as a child – the building up of opinions and shaping of ideas.

"It's my sexuality, and I have the right to express it. That doesn't make me cheap or unethical."

"There is unbelievable power in ownership, and women should own their sexuality. There is a double standard when it comes to sexuality that still persists.

Men are free, and women are not. That is crazy.

The old lessons of submissiveness and fragility made us victims. Women are so much more than that.

You can be a businesswoman, a mother, an artist, and a feminist – whatever you want to be – and still be a sexual being. It is not mutually exclusive."

– Beyoncé.

Your sexuality is your own statement, and no one should judge it. The way you look at yourself, dress and express yourself is your individual right. Be totally unapologetic about the way you are – it's your expression – unique and rare. Every person has the right to express and be himself/herself. Don't flinch to speak your mind, and don't budge from the way you speak, dress, express, behave, walk, smile, and above all, live your life.

This chapter is for every man in a woman, and the woman in every man.

We friends met after a long, long time, and everyone had transpired into this beautiful person nurtured by time, coming from different places, and living differently.

We sat down and had a few drinks – we truly spoke.

I shared, "Life is all about continuous transformation in each moment of your life. You change, and in your daily life, those moments of slow transformation go unnoticed. We rather brush off this gradual growth within us – we shirk off how we begin to respond, speak, and express. We are changing each moment. It's a beautiful process that happens with each human being – man, woman, lesbian, transgender, gay – just about anyone. We so conveniently neglect – there is a need to be more of yourself and be accepted for that."

Rupal started speaking bang on – she probably had seen through more than what we all had, and her experience was extremely personal.

"The world wouldn't always accept you the way you are, and that is where it all begins – the denial draws the rejection of being distinct."

Today, if I choose to dress up like a man, I'm mocked, and people stare at me. People don't stop at that – they comment, slur, tear you down, and that's gravely hurting. Given the fact that this is how I feel from within, that is why I'm who I am. It takes courage to stand up for yourself. If I express myself more like a man, what is bothering you?

We all were taken aback by her fury! Sagar was quietly listening to her – not like he used to be during his college days. But he chose to go and hug her. This was an emotional moment. It was an outburst that was waiting to happen. She just needed the right place and the people.

So be it; she did speak her mind. Something she had not done for years.

Rekha was dressed up beautifully in revealing clothes. We saw a few men ogling at her. Extremely gracious and beautiful. So we all began teasing her.

"You still look hot – look at all the men eyeing you!"

Now it was time for her to speak her mind. After all, what are friends meant for? To share your feelings!!

"There is great beauty in being you and expressing yourself. I love to wear short skirts and sexy clothes. I'm used to wearing makeup whenever I step out. I love to express my sexuality in such a way. Yes, I love to look at myself in the mirror when I'm all dressed and love myself this way. But whenever I walk out of my home, I have people ogling at me, and they make me so conscious about how I dress. I could have been discouraged and chosen to dress up not the way I chose to. But, I stick to my guns and define my style – rejecting everyone else who has no share in my individuality and sexuality."

She spoke powerfully, and she was in command. I still remember Rekha; a meek and silent girl while in college. It was a pleasure to witness this beautiful transformation – a realisation of her own sexuality. Probably as we grow up and face life, we all transform and find our innate being.

I was just thinking to myself:

"How much we have all changed? But how many of us have accepted ourselves for the way we are? Are we comfortable in our own skin? It's okay to be fat, it's okay to be extremely thin, it's okay to be short, and it's okay to be a lot taller."

It's all okay up to the point in time when you don't feel uncomfortable about yourself.

I agreed with Rekha,

"You know, guys, I would love to dance with a man or go have a cup of coffee with someone. That doesn't mean that 'I'm asking for it', or 'inviting someone', or 'I'm available'. Isn't it?

I can propose to a man rather than wait for a man to propose to me. Even the fact that I love holding someone's hands or hugging my best friend, who happens to be a man. It's all about my sexuality and the way I express my innate desires. Why should I be judged about such trivial things?

The younger generation is much more liberated and openly explores and expresses their sexuality. However, society still condemns open expression of one's sexuality.

In fact, after being a mother, the world starts looking at you differently. You are not supposed to express your sexuality openly because now you are going to mother a child. So, should I stop being a sexual being after giving birth to a child? It's my desire to be desirable. No one can judge me for that! Slut-shaming is still so common in our society where women or young girls are criticised for openly expressing their sexuality."

While we were all speaking a bit more about ourselves and our being, I got on the phone to search for this wonderful view that Sushmita Sen has about sexuality.

I actually blurted out,

"Hey guys, I've found this article a few days back and saved it. Let me read a part of it to you."

I love the way Sushmita Sen expresses herself!

"Sexiness is all about one's personality and attitude," Sushmita Sen mentioned in an article in India Today.

"Being sexy is a misconstrued definition. A sexy woman is supposed to be more of a woman than others. But it actually has to do with one's personality and attitude. It is not about baring. The sexiest people are those who are covered from head to toe. Sexiness is an inbuilt trait - everybody has it."

"Some of us repress it strongly in our childhood because of shyness or inhibition. It is also because we are constantly told by our families how to sit, talk, be cultured, and ladylike so that when we grow up, a decent man should want to marry us."

"But now people accept that you come of age when you recognise, accept, and are comfortable with your own sexuality.

Everyone wants to be with those who are ready to explore themselves rather than pretend to know what they don't."

Amar was so excited about this.

"Wow, wonderful! What a way to express it! I feel sex is only a part of us as sexual beings but an important one. We all are sexual beings. It is just the way we speak, sit, stand, look at someone, smile, flutter our eyes, dance, cry, and laugh. It's how we rejoice ourselves. Minute things about us show how we express our sexuality. It is at the heart of our being, what we do, what we believe in, along with the fact that how others respond to us."

Rukmini jumped out of her seat and rejoiced.

"Yes, yes, that is just what I have been feeling lately. You put it perfectly."

Our party ended on a great note, but I had a lot of reading to begin with on sexuality. It took me some time to understand a few vital things like sexual health and sensuality.

I'm sharing with you a bit of what I read.

The Department of Health in Iqaluit, Nunavut, explains about sexual health:

One of the main factors that influence sexual health is body image. It is about how you look at yourself and feel about your body in your own mind. Sometimes we might feel we are not beautiful enough, not tall enough, or not feminine enough. This thinking about self can get risky when making decisions about our sexual expression and lead to low self-esteem. In such cases, people think about what can be done to overcome this feeling.

Other important factors about sexual health are:

Our relationship experiences, intimacy, and love.

Never repress your sexuality – always be comfortable in your skin. It is important to be sexually healthy because it's at the heart of your being, who you are, what you believe in, how you feel, and how you respond to others.

"In India, the centuries-old stereotype that the man works and makes money, while the woman looks after him, has made men repressed. They are unable to enjoy equality or say, 'I'm tired. I want to take six months off. You take over.' He will still be a man. A man should be like a bamboo shoot, able to bend in a storm but not so rigid that it breaks him."

- Sushmita Sen (From the interview published in India Today, as mentioned above).

I also listened to a TED talk delivered by Mandy Ronda called 'Moving Beyond Sexual Shame'.

Let me share some quotes from her talk that speak directly about sexuality.

"What is healthy and positive sexuality?"

"It is the most potent form of life energy. It is the force by which we are all created. We are all literally made of it. It is a force by which we can create new life by ourselves. It is a source of health and happiness, passion, playfulness, pleasure, and power. It is a source of connection with your body, and the most beautiful intimate connection we can have with another human being.

But mostly, it is the ultimate expression of self-love because it's about daring to express yourself. It doesn't just happen in the bedroom. Your sexuality is an essential part of who you are and how you show up in the world. Feelings of shame, fear, and guilt are the biggest obstacles in living a joyful, pleasurable, and purposeful life."

So, we should not feel the urge to hide ourselves and not accept ourselves. Have the self-acceptance to express yourself as you are. Love yourself for who you are. It is possible to move beyond sexual shame for everyone."

- Mandy Ronda

In fact, the strongest relationship we have with ourselves is the sexual connection. We need not shun it. It's a beautiful journey of becoming and moving beyond shame about our sexuality.

Vidya Balan starred in a movie called 'Dirty Picture', and in her interview, she speaks about being comfortable in her skin.

She realised that if you develop a more positive relationship with your own body, then it has nothing to do with your size.

Famous actress Rekha spoke about sensuality too when asked, "What does it feel like to be sexy at 50?" in an article published in the Times of India.

Rekha's answer was,

"Sensuality is more like it. I am, therefore, I'm sensual. True sensuality is something that is inherent or innate. It cannot be acquired. It oozes out constantly without one's realising it."

Every woman has the innate power to express her sexuality. It's only undiscovered sometimes, and that is a grave injustice done to yourself.

Task:

Ask yourself,

Do I love my body?

Do I think being sexually expressive is a shame?

Do I love my naked body? Do I love my looks?

Whenever I dress up, do I look in the mirror and say, "I think I should not wear this loud makeup or tight T-shirt because people will pass comments or I will be judged?"

What is my sexuality?

This is your expression made for your own sake.

Positive self-talk

I'm a sexual being.

It is safe for me to express my sexuality.

I'm not ashamed of my sexuality and its expression.

I don't feel shameful about my body or sexual desires.

My sexual desire is my own, and I love to express it just the way I feel.

I accept my body, face, smile, behaviour, the way I talk, dance, sit, and dress.

I love wearing short skirts, makeup, long earrings, and heels.

I'm beautifully sensuous.

I will not shun my body or my sexuality.

My sexuality is unique, and I don't allow anyone to comment on it.

I have all the rights to express my sexuality. I love my body and mind the way they are.

References

(n.d.). Home: Marriage Counseling | Couples Therapy | Chesterfield, MO 63017. Retrieved November 15, 2024, from https://www.mmhcounseling.com/

(n.d.). https://www.facebook.com/ProudBhagavathi/photos/sanskrit-terms-used-by-the-husband-for-the-wife-were-pathni-the-one-who-leads-th/634898740694141/

(n.d.). https://www.news18.com/news/lifestyle/consciously-single-dating-trend-shows-how-more-women-are-comfortable-being-single-6770629.html

(n.d.). https://medium.com/@ayeshamuneer101/feminism-isnt-about-making-women-stronger-women-are-already-strong-it-s-about-changing-the-way-11f87fbe31ef

(n.d.). https://www.facebook.com/photo.php?fbid=1939661499420712&id=447263991993811&set=a.475172202536323

(n.d.). https://pure.uva.nl/ws/files/39692103/app.pdf

(n.d.). Musixmatch: The World's Largest Lyrics Catalog. Retrieved November 15, 2024, from https://www.musixmatch.com/

(n.d.). https://cimcyc.ugr.es/en/information/news/sacrifice-leaving-work-their-families-cost-benefit-analysis#:~:text=On%20the%20other%20hand%2C%20both,compared%20to%20their%20male%20partners.

(n.d.). Untitled. Retrieved November 16, 2024, from https://wjsmith.faculty.unlv.edu/smithtest/SHIVAwomenDevEcol.pdf

(n.d.). The Wire. https://thewire.in/women/gender-bias-under-five-mortality

(2023, Feb 26). Hindustan Times. https://www.hindustantimes.com/ht-newsletter/htmindthegap26022023.html

Anonymous was a Woman. (2022, March 1). HMCPL Online. Retrieved November 15, 2024, from https://blog.hmcpl.org/anonymous-was-woman

ARORA, P. (2024, March 8). Financial Independence: How women are increasingly taking financial decisions. The Economic Times. Retrieved November 15, 2024, from https://economictimes.indiatimes.com/markets/stocks/news/financial-independence-how-women-are-increasingly-taking-financial-decisions/articleshow/108330717.cms?from=mdr

Bach, R. (n.d.). Brainy Quote. https://www.brainyquote.com/quotes/richard_bach_389113

Barone, D. F. (n.d.). Reciprocity & Exchange: The Kula Ring Return. Human Relations Area Files. https://hraf.yale.edu/teach-ehraf/reciprocity-exchange-the-kula-ring/

'The saga of women's status in ancient Indian civilisation' Bhaswati Pal published in MISCELLANEA GEOGRAPHICA – REGIONAL STUDIES ON DEVELOPMENT

Bhugra, D. (n.d.). Sexual violence against women: Understanding cross-cultural intersections. PubMed. Retrieved November 15, 2024, from https://pubmed.ncbi.nlm.nih.gov/24082244/

Bonaparte, N. (n.d.). Quote by Napoleon Bonaparte: "Nothing is more difficult, and therefore more p..." Goodreads. Retrieved November 15, 2024, from https://www.goodreads.com/quotes/24866-nothing-is-more-difficult-and-therefore-more-precious-than-to

Brishti Guha (2015). The Moderns of Ancient India. Times of India. Retrieved November 25, 2024, from https://timesofindia.indiatimes.com/blogs/toi-edit-page/the-moderns-of-ancient-india/

ARORA, P. (2024, March 8). Financial Independence: How women are increasingly taking financial decisions. The Economic Times. Retrieved November 15, 2024, from https://economictimes.indiatimes.com/markets/stocks/news/financial-independence-how-women-are-increasingly-taking-financial-decisions/articleshow/108330717.cms?from=mdr

Bumble India and SEA's comms director Samarpita Samaddar moves on. (2024, April 3). Afaqs. Retrieved November 15, 2024, from https://www.afaqs.com/people-spotting/bumble-india-and-seas-comms-director-samarpita-samaddar-moves-on

Buser, T. (2019, July 9). Women give up competing more easily than men. LSE Blogs. Retrieved November 15, 2024, from https://blogs.lse.ac.uk/businessreview/2019/07/09/women-give-up-competing-more-easily-than-men/

Dr. Neff. K, 2021, Fierce Compassion, Harper Wale

publication year, book title (italicized), edition (if not the first), publisher, and sometimes the place of publication,

Clarke, S. (2014, April 9). Beyonce: 'Women Should Own Their Sexuality' - ABC News. ABC News. Retrieved November 16, 2024, from https://abcnews.go.com/blogs/entertainment/2014/04/beyonce-women-should-own-their-sexuality

Consciously Single and Happy. (n.d.). Pune Mirror. https://punemirror.com/pune/pune-speaks/consciously-single-and-happy/cid1673505398.htm

Consciously SINGLE and happy. (2023, Jan 12). PuneMirror Bureau.

A country like India has lot of potential. (n.d.). https://www.goodreads.com/quotes/7984357-a-country-like-india-has-a-lot-of-potential-i

Country needs to do a lot more for women empowerment in India: Sania. (n.d.). https://timesofindia.indiatimes.com/sports/tennis/top-stories/country-needs-to-do-lot-more-for-women-empowerment-in-sports-sania/articleshow/68863845.cms

COVID-19 impact on women and gender equality. (2020, July 15). McKinsey & Company. Retrieved November 15, 2024, from https://www.mckinsey.com/featured-insights/future-of-work/covid-19-and-gender-equality-countering-the-regressive-effects

Devastatingly pervasive: 1 in 3 women globally experience violence. (n.d.). the United Nations. Retrieved November 15, 2024, from https://www.un.org/africarenewal/news/devastatingly-pervasive-1-3-women-globally-experience-violence

Devastatingly pervasive: 1 in 3 women globally experience violence. (2021, March 9). World Health Organization (WHO). Retrieved November 15, 2024, from https://www.who.int/

news/item/09-03-2021-devastatingly-pervasive-1-in-3-women-globally-experience-violence

Dr. R Radha, 'Historical perspective of violence against women in India through various ages' published in 2019 in the Journal of Basic and Applied Research International.

81% women in India feel more at ease being unmarried, living alone: Study. (2023, January 8). WION. Retrieved November 15, 2024, from https://www.wionews.com/entertainment/lifestyle/news-_1-women-in-india-feel-more-at-ease-being-unmarried-living-alone-study-550444

Facts and figures: Ending violence against women. (n.d.). UN Women. Retrieved November 15, 2024, from https://www.unwomen.org/en/what-we-do/ending-violence-against-women/facts-and-figures

58% youth believe that men can dictate their women: MFF Survey. (n.d.). Business Today. https://www.business-standard.com/article/news-ani/58-youth-believe-that-men-can-dictate-their-women-mff-survey-119010700523_1.html

51% of women prefer low-risk FDs, only 7% invest in stocks: survey. (2024, January 15). Business Standard. Retrieved November 15, 2024, from https://www.business-standard.com/finance/personal-finance/51-of-women-prefer-low-risk-fds-only-7-invest-in-stocks-survey-124011500105_1.html

Jennings-Edquist, G. (2021, September 5) In a society that fetishises female self-sacrifice, saying 'no' saved me. The Guardian. Retrieved October 10, 2024 from https://www.theguardian.com/lifeandstyle/2021/sep/06/in-a-society-that-fetishises-female-self-sacrifice-saying-no-saved-me

Frayer, L., & Kumar, R. (2023, January 4). It's a mystery: Women in India drop out of the workforce even as the economy grows. NPR. Retrieved November 15, 2024, from https://www.npr.org/sections/goatsandsoda/2023/01/04/1146953384/why-women-in-india-are-dropping-out-the-workforce-even-as-the-economy-grows

Frayer, L., & Kumar, R. (2023, January 4). It's a mystery: Women in India drop out of the workforce even as the economy grows. NPR. Retrieved November 15, 2024, from https://www.npr.org/sections/goatsandsoda/2023/01/04/1146953384/why-women-in-india-are-dropping-out-the-workforce-even-as-the-economy-grows

Hill, N. (n.d.). Brainy Quote.

How early struggles in life shaped Mary Kom the boxer. (2021, July). https://olympics.com/en/news/how-early-struggles-in-life-shaped-mary-kom-the-boxer

https://www.india.com/news/india/over-96-per-cent-rape-cases-india-committed-by-persons-known-to-the-victims-ncrb-report-5613362/. (2022, September 22). India.com. https://www.india.com/news/india/over-96-per-cent-rape-cases-india-committed-by-persons-known-to-the-victims-ncrb-report-5613362/

https://www.indiatoday.in/magazine/cover-story/story/20040920-actress-former-miss-universe-sushmita-sen-speaks-about-sexuality-789359-2004-09-19. (n.d.). India Today. https://www.indiatoday.in/magazine/cover-story/story/20040920-actress-former-miss-universe-sushmita-sen-speaks-about-sexuality-789359-2004-09-19

I Am, Therefore I'm Sensual : Rekha. (2004, August 29). Times of India.

The Incredible Story of India's Revolutionary Feminist: Dr. Muthulakshmi Reddy (1886–1968). (2024, June 18). Cureus. https://www.cureus.com/articles/256584-the-incredible-story-of-indias-revolutionary-feminist-dr-muthulakshmi-reddy-1886-1968#!/

India lodged average 86 rapes daily, 49 offences against women per hour in 2021: NCRB data. (2022, August 31). The Hindu. Retrieved November 15, 2024, from https://www.thehindu.com/news/national/india-lodged-average-86-rapes-daily-49-offences-against-women-per-hour-in-2021-government-data/article65833488.ece

India Suffers Because Women Eat The Last And The Least. (2019, July 12). Outlook Business. Retrieved November 15, 2024, from https://www.outlookbusiness.com/opinions/india-suffers-because-women-eat-the-last-and-the-least-news-413250

Jackson, C. (n.d.). In their book, Women Don't Ask: Negotiation and the Gender Divide. UC Davis ADVANCE. Retrieved November 15, 2024, from https://ucd-advance.ucdavis.edu/post/women-dont-ask-negotiation-and-gender-divide

Babcock. L and Lara. L. (n.d.). In their book, Women Don't Ask: Negotiation and the Gender Divide. UC Davis ADVANCE. Retrieved November 15, 2024, from https://ucd-advance.ucdavis.edu/post/women-dont-ask-negotiation-and-gender-divide

Jelinek, J. (2023, November 20). Victim mentality: Causes, signs, and more. MedicalNewsToday. Retrieved November 15,

2024, from https://www.medicalnewstoday.com/articles/victim-mentality#causes

Jelinek, J. (2023, November 20). Victim mentality: Causes, signs, and more. MedicalNewsToday. Retrieved November 15, 2024, from https://www.medicalnewstoday.com/articles/victim-mentality

Kalia, S. (2022, August 5). Indian Women Hold Only 10% of Directing, Writing Positions in Films and TV: Report. The Swaddle. Retrieved November 15, 2024, from https://www.theswaddle.com/indian-women-hold-only-10-of-directing-writing-positions-in-films-and-tv-report

Kalia, S. (2022, August 5). Indian Women Hold Only 10% of Directing, Writing Positions in Films and TV: Report. The Swaddle. Retrieved November 15, 2024, from https://www.theswaddle.com/indian-women-hold-only-10-of-directing-writing-positions-in-films-and-tv-report

Kaur, R. (n.d.). Quote by Rupi Kaur: "what is the greatest lesson a woman should lear..." Goodreads. Retrieved November 15, 2024, from https://www.goodreads.com/quotes/8924540-what-is-the-greatest-lesson-a-woman-should-learn-that

Key data | UNICEF India. (n.d.). Unicef. Retrieved November 16, 2024, from https://www.unicef.org/india/key-data

Khushbu Sundar says she was abused by her father as a child in interview. (2023, March 6). The Hindu. Retrieved November 15, 2024, from https://www.thehindu.com/entertainment/khushbu-sundar-says-she-was-abused-by-her-father-as-a-child-in-interview/article66586758.ece

Kom, M. (n.d.). Brainy Quote. https://www.brainyquote.com/quotes/mary_kom_957403

Lennon, J. (n.d.). Brainy Quote.

Lesley Gore – You Don't Own Me. (n.d.). Genius. Retrieved November 15, 2024, from https://genius.com/Lesley-gore-you-dont-own-me-lyrics

Lewis, H. (2020, February 15). Fighting the tyranny of 'niceness': why we need difficult women. Retrieved July 2024, from https://www.theguardian.com/books/2020/feb/15/feminism-feminists-tyranny-niceness-complexity

LITTLE WOMEN - Official Trailer (HD). (2019, August 13). YouTube. Retrieved November 15, 2024, from https://www.youtube.com/watch?v=AST2-4db4ic

Live Your Dream Life, Make a Difference. (2023, December 8). The Dream Catcher: Live Your Dream Life, Make a Difference. Retrieved November 15, 2024, from https://thedreamcatch.com/reciprocity-in-relationships-why-we-need-to-stop-chasing-people-who-make-no-effort/

Mankani, S. (2020, November 13). Vidya Balan on embracing body positivity, and why acting is her dream job. Vogue India. Retrieved November 16, 2024, from https://www.vogue.in/magazine-story/vidya-balan-movies-roles-body-positivity-interview/

Maternal Mortality. (n.d.). https://www.who.int/news-room/fact-sheets/detail/maternal-mortality/

Medinipur or Midnapore. (n.d.). Wikipedia. Retrieved November 15, 2024, from https://en.wikipedia.org/wiki/Midnapore

The moderns of ancient India. (2015, December 25). Times of India. Retrieved November 15, 2024, from https://timesofindia.indiatimes.com/blogs/toi-edit-page/the-moderns-of-ancient-india/

Moving beyond sexual shame | Mandy Ronda | TEDxApeldoorn. (2019, May 3). YouTube. Retrieved November 16, 2024, from https://www.youtube.com/watch?v=iexyh3hcdwQ

Murthy, S. (n.d.). Brainy Quote. https://www.brainyquote.com/quotes/sudha_murty_1079130

Murthy, S. (n.d.). Story Of Sudha Murthy. CiteHR. Retrieved November 15, 2024, from https://www.citehr.com/105519-story-sudha-murthy.html

My Fellow Women please don't settle less. (n.d.). https://www.linkedin.com/pulse/my-fellow-women-please-dont-settle-less-pratibha-mahindru/

Nagarajan, R. (2022, October 5). Female IMR in India: India's female IMR drops to same level as males' | India News. Times of India. Retrieved November 15, 2024, from https://timesofindia.indiatimes.com/india/indias-female-imr-drops-to-same-level-as-males/articleshow/94629223.cms

Nagarajan, R. (2022, October 5). Female IMR in India: India's female IMR drops to same level as males' | India News. Times of India. Retrieved November 15, 2024, from https://timesofindia.indiatimes.com/india/indias-female-imr-drops-to-same-level-as-males/articleshow/94629223.cms

O Womaniya! 2022 Report Reveals Status of Female Representation in Indian Films. (2022, August 4). The Quint. Retrieved November 15, 2024, from https://www.thequint.com/entertainment/bollywood/o-womaniya-2022-report-reveals-state-of-female-representation-in-indian-entertainment#read-more

Pandit, A. (2022, June 14). 'Girls drop out of schools due to early marriage, house work' | India News. Times of India. Retrieved

November 15, 2024, from https://timesofindia.indiatimes.com/india/girls-drop-out-of-schools-due-to-early-marriage-house-work/articleshow/92195487.cms

Pasricha, S., & Rebello, L. (2000, February 2). IRON ABSORPTION AND ITS IMPLICATIONS ON STRATEGIES TO CONTROL IRON DEFICIENCY ANAEMIA. Indian Council of Medical Research. Retrieved November 16, 2024, from https://main.icmr.nic.in/sites/default/files/icmr_bulletins/bufeb00.pdf

Rawat, S. (2022, September 27). Relationship tips by Sudha Murty | Times of India. Times of India. Retrieved November 15, 2024, from https://timesofindia.indiatimes.com/life-style/books/web-stories/relationship-tips-by-sudha-murty/photostory/94486310.cms

Ray, B. (2023, September 5). "What we need as women is an equal seat at the table and to be heard". ET Hospitality. Retrieved November 15, 2024, from https://hospitality.economictimes.indiatimes.com/news/hotels/what-we-need-as-women-is-an-equal-seat-at-the-table-and-to-be-heard/103381223

Ray, B. (2023, September 5). "What we need as women is an equal seat at the table and to be heard". ET Hospitality. Retrieved November 15, 2024, from https://hospitality.economictimes.indiatimes.com/news/hotels/what-we-need-as-women-is-an-equal-seat-at-the-table-and-to-be-heard/103381223

Ream, A. D. (2010, July 12). Relationships and the Importance of Recipro... GoodTherapy.org. Retrieved November 15, 2024, from https://www.goodtherapy.org/blog/relationship-reciprocity/

Ronda, M. (2019, March). Moving beyond sexual shame. TEDxApeldoorn.

Sandoiu, A. (2019, August 15). Women no better at multitasking than men, study finds. MedicalNewsToday. Retrieved November 15, 2024, from https://www.medicalnewstoday.com/articles/326058

Sandomir, R. (2024, May 14). Ilon Specht, Who Empowered Women With 'I'm Worth It' Ad, Dies at 81. The New York Times. Retrieved November 15, 2024, from https://www.nytimes.com/2024/05/10/business/media/ilon-specht-dead.html

Savitribai Phule Jayanti 2024: Celebrating India's first woman teacher. (2024, January 3). Business Standard. Retrieved November 15, 2024, from https://www.business-standard.com/india-news/savitribai-phule-jayanti-2024-celebrating-india-s-first-woman-teacher-124010300302_1.html

Sawubona! (n.d.). Loom International. https://www.loominternational.org/sawubona/

Sengupta, A. (2024, January 17). 47% women take independent financial decisions, 51% prefer low-risk instruments: Report, ET BFSI. BFSI News. Retrieved November 15, 2024, from https://bfsi.economictimes.indiatimes.com/news/industry/47-women-take-independent-financial-decisions-51-prefer-low-risk-instruments-report/106916509

Sexiness is all about one's personality, attitude: Sushmita Sen. (2004, sept 20). India Today. https://www.indiatoday.in/magazine/cover-story/story/20040920-actress-former-miss-universe-sushmita-sen-speaks-about-sexuality-789359-2004-09-19

Sexuality Is. (n.d.). IRespectMyself. Retrieved November 15, 2024, from https://www.irespectmyself.ca/en/respect-yourself/healthy-sexuality/sexuality-is

Sudha Murty quotes on love, relationships, and marriage. (2024, March 10). Times of India. Retrieved November 15, 2024, from https://timesofindia.indiatimes.com/life-style/relationships/web-stories/sudha-murty-quotes-on-love-relationships-and-marriage/photostory/108346464.cms

Suri, S. (2022, May 9). Why Women Face More Food Insecurity Than Men. Retrieved November 16, 2024, from https://www.orfonline.org/research/why-women-face-more-food-insecurity-than-men

A Theory of Indebtedness. (n.d.). Springer Nature Link. https://link.springer.com/chapter/10.1007/978-1-4613-3087-5_1#:~:text=Democritus%2C%20for%20one%2C%20offered%20the,on%20his%20debt.%E2%80%9D%20Although%20the

The Truth about Single Women in India. (n.d.). Peter McGraw. https://petermcgraw.org/the-truth-about-single-women-in-india

The Truth About Single Women In India. (2023, August 3). Peter McGraw. https://petermcgraw.org/the-truth-about-single-women-in-india

Venkatasubramanian, S. (2024, August 29). Watch: She left a legacy | The remarkable tale of Dr. Muthulakshmi Reddy. The Hindu. Retrieved November 15, 2024, from https://www.thehindu.com/news/national/watch-the-remarkable-tale-of-dr-muthulakshmi-reddy/article68580577.ece

Victim Mentality. (n.d.). https://www.medicalnewstoday.com/articles/victim-mentality#definition

Vidya Balan reveals how her relationship with body image and desires has evolved through The Dirty Picture: 'I have always enjoyed intimacy' | Hindi Movie News. (2024, April 25). Times of India. Retrieved November 15, 2024, from https://timesofindia.indiatimes.com/entertainment/hindi/bollywood/news/vidya-balan-reveals-how-her-relationship-with-body-image-and-desires-has-evolved-through-the-dirty-picture-i-have-always-enjoyed-intimacy/articleshow/109601780.cms

Women's nutrition - UNICEF DATA. (n.d.). UNICEF Data. Retrieved November 15, 2024, from https://data.unicef.org/topic/nutrition/womens-nutrition/

Women's nutrition - UNICEF DATA. (n.d.). UNICEF Data. Retrieved November 15, 2024, from https://data.unicef.org/topic/nutrition/womens-nutrition/

Women's wellbeing and the burden of unpaid work. (2021, August 31). PubMed Central. Retrieved November 15, 2024, from https://www.ncbi.nlm.nih.gov/pmc/articles/PMC8406085/

Women no better at multitasking than men, study finds. Medical News Today. Retrieved December 10, 2024, from https://www.medicalnewstoday.com/articles/326058

https://www.youtube.com/watch?v=iexyh3hcdwQ

https://www.youtube.com/watch?v=AST2-4db4ic